WILDERNESS
TALES

WILDERNESS TALES

Adventures in the Backcountry

PETER CHRISTENSEN

VICTORIA · VANCOUVER · CALGARY

Heritage House Publishing Company Ltd.   Heritage House Publishing Company Ltd.
#108 – 17665 66A Avenue   PO Box 468
Surrey, BC V3S 2A7   Custer, WA
www.heritagehouse.ca   98240-0468

Library and Archives Canada Cataloguing in Publication
Christensen, Peter, 1951–
    Wilderness tales: adventures in the backcountry / Peter Christensen.—1st Heritage House ed.

ISBN 978-1-894974-70-7

    1. Christensen, Peter, 1951– —Anecdotes. 2. Outdoor life—Rocky Mountains, Canadian
(B.C. and Alta.)—Anecdotes. 3. Park rangers—Rocky Mountains, Canadian (B.C. and Alta.)—
Anecdotes. I. Title.

GV191.52.C47A3 2009   796.5092   C2008-908135-8

Originally published 2006 by Altitude Publishing Canada Ltd.

Library of Congress Control Number: 2009920308

Series editor: Lesley Reynolds.
Cover design: Chyla Cardinal. Interior design: Frances Hunter.
Cover photo: Peter Christensen at Lower Findlay Creek, by Mike Gall.

Mixed Sources
Cert no. SW-COC-001271
© 1996 FSC
FSC

The interior of this book was printed on 100% post-consumer recycled paper,
processed chlorine free and printed with vegetable-based inks.

Heritage House acknowledges the financial support for its publishing program from the Government
of Canada through the Book Publishing Industry Development Program (BPIDP), Canada Council
for the Arts and the province of British Columbia through the British Columbia Arts Council and the
Book Publishing Tax Credit.

BRITISH COLUMBIA
ARTS COUNCIL
Supported by the Province of British Columbia

The Canada Council | Le Conseil des Arts
for the Arts | du Canada

12 11 10 09   1 2 3 4 5

Printed in Canada

Top of the World Park Log Book
October 2, 1995 A.M. Clear

They say the only thing that stands between you
and the perfect run is fear—fear of failure.

What you should really be afraid of is what you'll
miss if you don't try. So, sell the house, sell the
Buick, sell everything; but don't sell out.

No matter how many times you crash, get up;
point the tips downtown and let 'em run.

There's no feeling on earth like living on the fall line.

Doug Johnson

Contents

Prologue

AS EVENING APPROACHED, JOE AND I *rode down the back trail of Stoney Mountain on our return from a nine-day shift in the backcountry. As we rounded the belly of the mountain we could at once hear the high-pitched buzzing sound of truck and car tires on the Trans-Canada Highway.*

After a shift in the backcountry where the soft thud of horses' feet, the twittering of a flock of cedar waxwings or the low moan of a wolf were everyday sounds, this roar of traffic was a stark reminder that we were returning to another time and another world. Hearing the white noise of the highway, I turned in my saddle, grinned at Joe and shouted, "It's the sound of civilization!"

Joe grinned back, understanding my meaning and the

contradictions inherent in the life we led. While working in the protected areas of the backcountry, we were not only insulated from the intrusions of highway noise, but from the stress of modern life. Time slowed down out there. It was as if we entered a different dimension.

Sometimes we would ride for three or four consecutive days to a destination, covering 25 to 40 kilometres of rugged mountain country per day. Time in the saddle had a rhythm of its own, as we constantly searched for signs of wildlife, cut trail and occasionally repacked after long, steep descents. Life progressed at about 5 kilometres an hour.

I threw my gear in the back of the truck and jumped into the cab. I fired up Old Red and eased out of the yard, making a right turn onto the Trans-Canada Highway. After the first kilometre I noticed the traffic whizzing by at an astounding rate; I also noted that I was driving about 70 kilometres an hour.

I have been at this juncture between backcountry and frontcountry pace many times. I take a deep breath, check and adjust my rear-view mirror, straighten up, check my speedometer, pay attention and then get with the traffic. I shift both mechanical and mental gears into high and enter the 21st century of daily hot baths, box-spring mattresses, constant multifaceted stimulus, and Laz-Z-Boy chairs.

1

A Horse
Named Wasp

DURING THE 1970S AND EARLY 1980S, I worked for various guide outfitting operations in British Columbia and the Yukon. After a dozen years of guiding in our spectacular wilderness Crown lands, I decided to make a change and applied for what seemed to me to be the best job in the federal Parks Service—working as ranch hand and remote area trail crew in the eastern ranges of the Alberta Rockies. After an intensive formal interview with senior warden staff, a hands-on evaluation by Banff National Park head horseman Johnny Nylund and waiting a year for a job offer, I was finally given a post as Remote Area Trail Crew Lead Hand. A great-sounding title!

Operations for this position were based out of the Banff

corrals at the foot of Cascade Mountain. Since I lived in
Radium Hot Springs, an hour-and-a-half drive south, I was
allowed a spot near the barns and corrals to park my sturdy
and comfortable 1962 Safeway camper trailer. As there had
been a rash of thefts from the barns and a number of new
and expensive saddles stolen, I think they figured having
someone camped part-time near the barns was a good idea.
This became my spring, summer and early fall base camp
for the next five years.

On the trail crew, we worked nine days in mountain
backcountry and five days out, from mid-May to mid-October.
Typically, my working partner, Joe, and I would buy
groceries in Banff Monday evening, have a beer or two
at Wild Bill's Saloon to compare notes with other park
employees and on Tuesday morning head out to the wild
and magnificent backcountry of the Rockies front ranges
to maintain the trails and remote warden patrol stations in
Banff National Park.

Joe and I would return the following Wednesday afternoon and turn our five-horse cavalcade into the home
corrals, where they would have all the hay they could eat
and a big ration of oats and kibbles once a day for the
next five rest days. The corrals were a buggy location
during the summer, so despite the rest and bountiful
rations, I believe the horses were happy to see us when
we returned for the next shift and just as anxious to "get
out of Dodge" as we were.

The Banff district has 16 backcountry warden stations and many hundreds of kilometres of interconnecting trails linking the stations, remote destinations and public campgrounds. Each station is a neat little homestead in the middle of a wilderness paradise, usually consisting of a small, well-outfitted cabin just right for a couple of people, a storage barn supplied during the winter by skidoo with oats and hay, and a corral, all situated near good grazing pastures and a creek. After years of guiding and sleeping on the ground under leaking tent walls in dubious weather, staying in a warm, dry cabin at the end of a day's work outside was a welcome relief.

As ranch hands, we provided the support and services necessary to keep the backcountry facilities and trails in shape. In days gone by, wardens used to do this type of work as well as their enforcement and public safety duties, but many of the new '80s wardens didn't like to get dirty or develop callouses on their hands. For many of them, the only sweat on their brows was from spending too many days hunched over computers generating models and predictions based on flawed mathematics. Not necessarily to the wardens' liking, in the postmodern age of process politics, the federal Liberals deemed that wardens should spend their time providing "scientific" data to justify their existence.

From time to time, the chief park warden and his vice-presidents and a few selected businesspeople from Banff would parade the backcountry on a helicopter-assisted "Musical Ride," while the old-fashioned-type backcountry wardens made regular patrols throughout the district. When more than a day's ride from town, we saw few people. It was our job as remote area trail crew to keep trails cleared, cabins repaired and stocked with split firewood and kindling, barns, corrals and gates functional, and help with packing goods or hauling horses in support of the park's backcountry operations. It was, in the words of an old-timer, "good honest work."

Joe was a fine partner. He grew up in Banff and worked on the park trail crews in his teens. His father had worked for the Parks Service. Joe was a talented hockey player as a lad and in his early 20s played in the European leagues and farm teams. Though he was a capable player, he didn't have the temperament for blood sport. After a few seasons Joe realized that as a player he was "just meat for business." He decided to return to the mountains and become a warden. He went to college and did the obligatory courses in resource management and enforcement and then began running the hoops necessary to acquire a warden job with the feds. In the interim, he worked summers as my partner on the trail crew.

Joe and I worked well together. He knew the work from his earlier trail crew experience, and he had a strong work ethic. Perhaps because of his athletic background and abilities, he loved the physical work, and unlike many backcountry partners who get thrown together, Joe and I got along. At the base of our friendship was a deep love of the country and of what we were doing.

I have worked with many people in the backcountry and not all were happy to be there. At first they would be enthusiastic, caught up in the romance of the wilderness, but after a few days without hot showers, TV and the constant digital stimulus of the modern era their spirits would sag. They would become sulky about the work and worry about missing a meeting or some social event.

Maybe to live and work in the bush you need by nature to be satisfied with silence or the sound of a river. Some say you need to be at peace with yourself, especially since you and your "self" are going to be spending so much uninterrupted time together. I do know that you need to be intensely interested in your surroundings to enjoy the backcountry.

After each shift Joe and I would check in at the warden office with our supervisor, Gord, to talk about work completed, what was to be accomplished next shift and to pick up our paycheques from dispatch.

Dispatch is the control centre at the warden office, where dispatch staff process all emergency calls, check-ins and correspondence. One day late in the season, back from the bush after a regular nine-day shift, we were chatting good-naturedly before heading out the door for our days off.

To our surprise one of the women at dispatch suddenly asked us, "Why do you guys get along so well?" We turned to face her. The question took both of us by surprise and we looked at her quizzically.

She continued, "I mean you've just spent nine days together in the bush and you're still happy. Everybody else that goes out together comes back enemies. What's the secret?"

Joe thought for a moment and then said, "We don't talk."

"What do mean, you don't talk?"

"We don't talk. That's why we get along." We both smiled, satisfied with the answer, and headed out, leaving a somewhat perplexed dispatcher at her desk. "See ya next time," Joe called back.

I had not considered this lack of talk unusual till then. Long days in the saddle with a bunch of horses strung out between us, or noisy, concentrated work with chainsaws and hand tools did not facilitate nor require the constant flapping of gums. In the evenings I was tired and at ease with doing a day's work so I figured why spoil the pregnant song of a varied thrush or the lazy sounds of a river with chatter. And I guess Joe felt the same.

Hauling Horses

Sometimes we worked out of the Ya Ha Tinda Ranch. The Ya Ha Tinda is one of the few genuine horse ranches left in the country. It had its origins in 1908 when the famous Brewster brothers of Banff leased the land for winter pasture for their pack strings. The area was originally included in the federal Rocky Mountain Park of the day, and the grazing lease was later taken over by the feds in 1917.

Though excluded from the park by boundary changes in 1930, the 4,000-hectare Ya Ha Tinda is still owned and operated by Banff National Park. Horses have been bred, raised and trained there for the warden service since 1917.

Ya Ha Tinda means "mountain prairie" in Stoney dialect. It is thought small bands of Native peoples from the prairies migrated through this area annually until recent times. Archaeological evidence of people in the area dates back 9,400 years. It is an isolated but habitable prairie bounded to the northeast and south by forested foothills and on the west by the limestone front range of the Rockies. It is about a five-hour drive from Banff, located just north and east of where the Red Deer River cascades out of the front range beneath Warden Rock.

Today the Ya Ha Tinda area of rolling, grassy foothills sparsely covered in pine, spruce and aspen is one of the largest elk-wintering areas in Alberta. Grizzly bear, cougar, wolf, moose, deer, elk and mountain sheep thrive in the montane environment. The ranch currently runs a string of brood mares and studs and winters about 170 horses, many of which are used to patrol the western parks during spring, summer and fall.

The first job of the spring season was to truck 70 head of horses fresh off Ya Ha Tinda winter range down the Forestry Trunk Road to Banff. The horses would be shod and several moved to warden stations throughout the mountain park system for use during the summer.

I looked forward to visiting and working at the Ya Ha Tinda as the ranch's long history, great beauty and isolation appealed to me.

The Parks Service owned a couple of aging, park-yellow, five-tonne flatbed trucks fitted with stock racks. Johnny, the head horseman, set a fierce pace up the winding Forestry Trunk Road through the Alberta foothills to the ranch, but I had driven time-is-money gravel trucks at high speeds on country roads as a kid, and I was hot on his tail up the many kilometres of banked, soft-shouldered gravel road.

After a rattling four-hour chase, we pulled up to the ranch gate at the same time and got out to open the gates. The yellow park trucks stood sweating and steaming in the frosty air. We lit smokes. As usual, Johnny had little to say and with a grin on his face climbed back into his cab as if he was mounting a rode-out bronc. We ground our way on a rough lane up the last hill into the ranch yard.

As we reached the barn and loading ramps, ranch foreman Cal Hayes, a short, stocky, bow-legged man in his early 60s, strutted down from the headquarters cabin like a bantam rooster and announced that coffee was on and we should join him and the boys right away.

It was not so much an invitation as an order, but after the long drive from Banff we readily complied. Over coffee, Steve and Kenny, the two ranch cowboys, and I listened earnestly to Johnny and Cal's gossip about the various wardens and other "parkies," the horses and the latest knothead idea from head office in Calgary.

After coffee, we sauntered down to the barn, where 70 horses fresh off winter range were milling around excitedly in a round corral attached to the barn. The edgy horses sniffed the air, sensing a change. They were restless and snapped at each other; putting them in such close quarters had broken the established pecking order, personal space and group dynamics.

Cal, dressed in his best Carhartt chore coat, white shirt and bright red bandana, began barking orders, and we lined up the trucks to the loading ramps and grabbed a handful of halters.

Steve, a young and talented horse trainer, made a short run at the two-metre-high corral fence and vaulted over the top rail in a handspring, landing nimble as a cat on the other side. He pulled a couple of halters from under the lower rail, hung them on his arm and waited for instructions.

Cal was an old-time cowboy, tough and rough, not only around the edges but clean through; he had lots of savvy and suffered no fools. I was nervous around Cal, a feeling I think he enjoyed and cultivated in apprentices. He ruled the Ya Ha Tinda with absolute authority. It didn't need to be said—his way or the highway.

Once I helped him hot brand a horse and after the iron had burned the sheep's head brand (Banff park's brand is a silhouette of a bighorn ram) deep onto the left foreshoulder of a big bay horse, Cal asked, "Did you touch him?"

"Touch him?" I queried.

"We touched him alright," confirmed Cal. I knew he didn't mean just his hide. Once the sheep's head brand was on a government horse it was never sold.

But Cal wasn't mean, just practical from living a life of horses, mountains, cowboys, history and weather. He was not above stirring the pot, though, just to see what would happen. So rather than letting the 70 head of wary winter horses settle down and be caught out one at a time, Cal slipped into the corral and planted himself in the centre of the pen.

With a widening grin on his churlish face, he whirled a buzzing rope till all 70 head were charging in a circle—kicking, snorting and bucking. We stared in amazement as Steve, caught slightly off guard by so much action, made the mistake of moving a little too far into the circle. As the horses milled and crowded into the back of the pen, Tucker, a big, dark chestnut gelding, bolted past Steve, reached out with a hind foot and whacked him in the ribs. You could hear the hollow thud. Steve winced, surprised and knowing. At first he tried not to let it show, but anyone could see that Tucker had hurt him.

"What happened?" asked Cal as Steve held his hand and arm across his chest and grimaced.

"Tucker you sonofabitch." Tucker heard his name and turned a wild eye to Cal. Steve left the corral quietly, grimacing slightly as I opened the gate for him, and walked slowly up toward the bunkhouse. Later that summer I heard Tucker had cracked a couple of Steve's ribs. Anyway, it sure slowed him down!

Johnny and I waited till the herd settled a bit and then went in and caught 10 horses. One at a time we led them out to the trucks and tied them in head to tail, standing room only, and forced the rear gate of the stock racks shut behind them. We quickly gathered spare halters and threw them into the passenger side of the cab. The restless horses kicked at the sides of the racks but couldn't move as they were so jammed together.

"Better get going before they kick the damn sides out," Johnny said. We started the engines and ground our way slowly down the long hill to the ranch gate. Better to get moving so the horses had to fight for balance instead of wrestling with each other or the confinement.

From the ranch we followed a slow road of washouts, washboard and soft shoulders till we hit the Forestry Trunk Road at the bridge over the Red Deer River. We stopped at the Mountain Aire Lodge for coffee to go, then drove back to Banff in earnest. Cold rain and wind pelted the shifting load of horses, and hot engines strained as we wound our way south through the wind-whipped pine forests of the east slopes.

The winding road, dark spring storms and restless horses seemed to complement each other as we careened through hills and curves and across bridges. Long, skinny lodgepole pines swung back and forth in unison and wind gusts buffeted the truck.

After Morley we were back on the Trans-Canada and the last hour of the run to the Banff corrals. Long pillars of dark rain streaked out of the front ranges toward us, and easterlies buffeted the truck. I glanced at the horses in the rear-view mirror—heads held high and manes tossed like breakers on a rough sea.

Running in the blood of those horses was thousands of years of evolution. First domesticated around 3,000 BC in the Karma Kum desert of present-day Turkmenistan, these incredible animals have served in war and peace as friend, slave and partner. Until only 100 years ago the horse was man's primary means of land transportation and power. The horse pulled our agricultural equipment and took us wherever we needed to go; we rode him to war and for sport. The horse enabled civilization to expand.

The incongruity of 10 horses jammed into a small corral on a set of wheels doing 110 kilometres an hour down an asphalt strip surrounded by gasoline tankers and cars struck me as a strange and unholy meeting of the past and present. I felt like I was hauling a load of living history into a hostile present.

In Banff we backed into the loading ramps, opened the doors to the confined horses and untied them one at a time. They charged into the familiar corral, rolled in the heavy sand and then headed out to the pasture shaking dust and sand from their backs. Tomorrow and the day after that we would make the same trip for another 20 horses.

Have You Got Him Conquered?

Because I had some experience packing and riding in the remote mountains, I was considered a decent find as a ranch hand and was deemed to have some skill. This had disadvantages as well as advantages. On the one hand, you'd be given some leeway in the way you did things, but on the other hand, more was expected of you. Every outfit I have worked for has a particular way of doing things, and Parks Canada was no different. I was yet to savvy the ways of Parks Canada's warden service, but would after a time come to appreciate their approach to horsemanship and safety as it was far more advanced than most outfits.

Johnny Nylund was more than a capable man with horses. He had grown up chasing wild ones in the foothills and knew horses and horse husbandry inside out. He was long on common sense and short on fools and had seen his share of "pilgrims" come and go.

"Pilgrims," as Johnny called them, came to the mountains to try another way of life, to try a little adventure. Only time would reveal whether or not the new arrivals would prove worthy, and Johnny had seen enough come and go that he was not likely to open up to anybody. At least, not for a long time and then only a little bit.

As head horseman at Banff, Johnny was in charge of the management and maintenance of corrals, barns, tack, hauling equipment and the general health of the herd. Together with the backcountry supervisor, he decided who would ride which horse. I was assigned a green-broke gelding named Wasp as a saddle horse.

"All he needs is miles. That's what they all need!" Johnny claimed. I suspected he was referring to both man and beast.

Wasp was a short-coupled quarter horse, three years old, light in the front end and a little small-boned for mountain work. But he was handsome with a beautiful blond coat and dark mane and tail. He had a dark stripe running down his backbone, a telltale sign of high-strung breeding lolling around in his blood. Over the next five years, Wasp would teach me some crucial lessons in horsemanship and life. I would eventually conclude that I, however, never taught Wasp a thing; he was born knowing a lot more about being a horse than I would ever know.

I would also come to say, "Working with horses taught me more about people than working with people." I have recited this aphorism among the so-called postmodern folk and was at first surprised that they were insulted; they seemed to feel they were being compared in an unsavoury way to an animal (forgetting that's what they are).

Their looks of disdain seemed to say, "How could anybody be so stupid to think they'd learned something about people from an animal?" After a time I came to expect they

24

would be insulted at the comparison and stopped sharing my hard-won wisdom. To my way of thinking, though, I had complimented both them and the horse.

The horses trained at the Ya Ha Tinda were named according to a letter of the alphabet that matched the year they were born. So all the "A" horses, with names like Aspen, Art, Albert or Abe, were born in the same year. This way the horse's age could be easily tracked, and just by knowing a horse's name you'd have some basic information about your future partner.

Over the years I learned that horses are either given or earn appropriate names. For instance, a horse named Bandit might be fond of stealing things or be a bit of a trickster. Arrogance or denial are terrible teachers and the first mistake I made was thinking that a young horse like Wasp couldn't have earned his name yet. I didn't see the name as reason for caution.

The first time I rode Wasp, my wife, Yvonne, and I were headed up to Stoney Cabin via Elk Pass. At the beginning of every trip into the backcountry there are a few very busy hours. Food and supplies must be packed carefully into boxes, tack checked over and horses brushed and steadied while they are saddled. Only then is the string ready for the journey. Leaving civilization behind is a gradual process.

At last we were ready to go. I carefully rechecked Wasp. I did not want to make any mistakes around this young horse that might lead to future bad habits.

I climbed aboard and walked and trotted him for a few minutes, then led him out of the corral and picked up the lead rope of the waiting pack string standing loaded and tied outside the corral. I led out on an old service road that turns into a well-built trail that circumnavigates Stoney Mountain. We made our way through a maze of ski-lift lines, huts and gondola cars, across Mt. Norquay ski hill, picked up a well-used hiking trail to Forty Mile Creek and took the junction to Elk Pass. Things had gone well with the young horse, considering all the obstacles we had passed.

As the vestiges of civilization slowly thin out, a moment comes when you realize that for the next few days there will be only high country, pristine forests, wildlife and horses. Evening will come slow. It is the beginning of a long, wonderful meditation free from exhaust fumes, noise and pavement. Free from ambitious, nattering bureaucrats and their reorganizations, centralizations and decentralizations. At these moments I take a deep breath and a good look at how lucky I am, at the sky, the forest, back at the string of horses behind, then let out a sigh and leave the bullshit behind for a while.

When we reached Elk Pass, Yvonne and I stopped for a bite to eat. Like many alpine passes, Elk Pass opens into a large meadow. Since we were in the open and on new horses on our first trip, we didn't let the horses go or tie them up, but stood by them hanging on to their lead shanks as they chewed on alpine grasses and scrub birch and willow.

A Horse Named Wasp

Watching a water pipit bounce from grass tuft to grass tuft looking for seeds, we quickly munched down ham sandwiches and sucked on juice boxes. I stuffed the lunch containers back in my saddlebag. I didn't know exactly how long it would take to reach Stoney Cabin so I didn't want to waste time.

I took the reins in hand and swung my leg briskly over Wasp's saddle. As I slipped into place I felt Wasp stiffen along his back and hunch down, then quickly spring up like a cat, down again, then up. Before I could find my stirrups or get my bearings, I was lying in the brush, holding the reins and considering the words Johnny had called out to me before I left the corral, "Have you got him conquered?"

"What?"

"Have you got him conquered?" he repeated. I had mumbled something like, "I guess so," then rode off. The truth is I hadn't given those words much thought at the time, just got on, picked up the pack string and rode out wondering what in hell he was talking about. But as I lay among the willows looking up at Wasp browsing on the brush and at the string of high cumulus clouds drifting across the late spring sky, it seemed like a good question.

Wasp was "all horse," as Johnny put it, and that spring day I received my first humbling lesson in what was the beginning of a five-year apprenticeship—one where Wasp gave me a considerable number of pointers in horsemanship, patience and respect for equines.

After that initial ride, Wasp bucked every morning for the next three years. It became a ritual. I would go out before breakfast and catch the horses. I would saddle Wasp and tie him up, saddle and load the pack string, have a "stirrup cup" (that last cup of coffee before you ride out), then, with the reins and lead shank in my left hand, I'd face Wasp toward the lead pack horse and slip quickly into the saddle and stirrups.

I faced the pack string when getting on because of a disastrous story I had heard about a packer working up north. Like many riders, this packer had climbed on his horse with it facing the same direction as his pack string. As he climbed on, he'd thrown the lead shank into the air and swung his leg over. In doing so he managed to throw a half hitch around his boot. The tangled rope slammed down on the offside of his horse, jerking the lead shank to the pack horse. The pack horse hauled back violently, pulling him out of the saddle. Unfortunately the packer's right foot caught in his riding horse's stirrup. The long and the short of it is that he was torn nearly in two and did not live to tell the tale. A gruesome thought.

Wasp and I would travel merrily along in the crisp morning air for 200 to 400 metres. Then I'd feel Wasp arch his back under my saddle, stretch and lift his tail, and take a dump. As soon as I felt him arching his back, I'd reach down, keeping the reins in my right hand, and grab the saddle horn with the same hand. I would tighten my thighs and wrap my calves around him and hang on. Then, as those golden buns of semi-digested hay dropped down onto his hocks, he would begin to run and buck wildly, leaving the pack string and my partner far behind.

A horse moving forward and going into a buck is not that hard to ride if you are forewarned. First, I'd lose the pack string lead rope, and as I held onto the saddle horn like the head of a snake poised to strike, I'd reach forward and grasp the left rein, pulling him sideways, trying to take the energy out of all that inspired horse flesh, meanwhile yelling whoa or some such nonsense.

We'd come to a stop down the trail a piece, turn around, and jog placidly back to where my partner Joe would be grinning from ear to ear—just slightly wider than the snickering pack horses. For the rest of the day things would go fairly well.

A Smart and Nimble Horse

Wasp had many talents. Approaching a gate, he would without hesitation or instruction side-pass up to the gate, wait patiently as you slid the rails back, then move through the gate with the pack string following, make a small circle and return, stop at the other side of the gate and wait patiently again while you reached down and slid the rail back in place. A nice time saver! Plus, I have also learned that generally the safest place while manoeuvring on or around a bunch of horses is on horseback, rather than in among the restless crowd.

29

If I had to get off to do trail work, I would simply drop the reins and Wasp would stay put grazing at the edge of the trail and not allow the pack horses to move past him. He would also stay reins up if told to do so by a short pull on the reins. I could then work down the trail swinging an axe or grub hoe, or running a chainsaw. When I clucked, Wasp would move the pack string up to where I was working and wait again. Once you've tried to swing an axe or run a chainsaw with a horse slobbering down your neck and generally trying to push you around, you realize how handy a smart horse like Wasp can be.

A smart and nimble horse can also be a good thing around bears, which you are bound to run into if you spend enough time in their territory. I have travelled in bear country for 25 years and seen many bears, but luckily I have felt threatened only once. Generally, you can avoid most confrontations by keeping a keen eye to the trail for fresh signs of bear and paying attention to what the extraordinary senses of your horse are telling you.

While riding down the Dormer Shortcut trail, a couple of days' ride north of Banff, I ran into a disgruntled young grizzly. Joe and I had met this same bruin a few days before in the upper Dormer along a noisy creek, but were able to move away and give him lots of space before he saw us. We had heard there was a young male in a bad mood in the area, probably the result of being pushed out of his home territory by larger, aggressive males or females.

We were paying particular attention as we moved through a patch of high willows along the noisy creek. We had seen fresh bear scat on the trail and noted rocks and logs that had been recently turned over.

At fairly close range, about 30 metres, the young, stone-grey grizzly stood up where we could easily see him. Waving his huge head back and forth, he sniffed the air, sampling the breeze from different angles. Because the creek generated a strong downwind and the bear was close to the creek, the irritable fellow was unable to get a fix on our scent and we were afforded time to move away.

My survival strategy, aside from paying attention to where I am and what I see, has been to move away as soon as I see a bear. It is my opinion and others' that bears are far more intense about personal space than we humans are. While clever humans will mask their smells with deodorant to prevent triggering aggressive behaviour should they be jammed in an elevator with other males of the species, grizzly bears have no such defence armaments. And should unwary or curious pilgrims invade a bear's personal space by accident or otherwise, there is a good chance the bear will react by charging and possibly attacking if they feel threatened. This behaviour has ensured the grizzly's place at the top of the wilderness food chain in the mountain country of western Canada. It is only in recent years that animal behaviourists have discerned the body language of bears to the degree that some predictability is possible.

The one time I felt threatened by a bear was when the situation on the Dormer Shortcut gave no easy retreat for either the bear or myself. I was leading and making good time riding Wasp down and around a sharp curve along a steep mountainside. As usual, two pack horses were strung together behind me, and Joe followed close behind them, leading an additional pack horse. At the point where the steep trail disappears into the thick forest above the Dormer River, the same young, male, dun-coloured grizzly we had seen the previous day was making his way up the trail.

It was a standoff. There was no easy way out. The horses were jamming up behind me and pushing Wasp down the trail toward the bear as they slowed and stopped. I waited. We had come around the curve near an opening in the forest. The bear stood his ground about 10 metres away; his head was low to the ground and swaying. Not a good sign. He did not want to give way. There was no doubt that it was our irritable friend from yesterday.

After a long minute, the bear turned uphill into a patch of small pines and I breathed a sigh of relief. Then he turned and started down the hill toward me. I could see saliva dripping from his curled lips. I could hear his teeth grinding and clicking. Another bad sign! And while it is true that I didn't have the greater awareness of bear body language that is now common knowledge, the 200 kilograms of meanness, bared teeth and flashing claws bearing down on me did not require in-depth interpretation to understand its meaning.

In nature, there's a point where animals make a group decision and act as one spontaneously. We have all witnessed how a flock of birds or a herd of deer suddenly moves away in unison.

In an instant, Wasp spun on his talented heels, dove down off the steep trail onto the shale-covered slope, and turned to head back up the trail from where we had come. With one foot in the stirrup and hanging far to the inside, I kept Wasp from rolling down the steep terrain. I galloped past Joe and the pack string looking like an accomplished trick rider, but knowing I was simply hanging on for dear life as we gained the trail behind the last pack horse. The pack string, not amused at my sacrificing them to the bear, formed into a mad mess while turning around on the trail, and once pointed up, galloped up the mountainside at full speed behind Wasp and me.

When the seven of us reached a point a ways up the slope, out in the open and far from the vengeful grizzly, all the horses came to a standstill in a circle looking in. This I assumed was the horses' natural defence response; all those lethal, shod back feet were now faced out and ready to do business. On the inside of the circle both men and horses showed a rather different demeanor. With eyes wide as tea saucers and pie plates, respectively, our faces plainly expressed, "Wow, that was close!"

Savvy

I have thought back to those days riding for the sheep's head brand with great fondness. I came to ride for the brand thinking I knew a bit about horses and packing, and I guess I knew some things. But the east-slope cowboys who worked under Cal Hayes or Johnny Nylund were great all-round, solid horsemen. Admittedly, Johnny wasn't much of a teacher, nor did he have a formal education, but I venture there's not too much about horses and horsemanship you couldn't learn from him by watching and doing what you were told.

And you couldn't take to heart his gruffness when you made a mistake—like the time I was hungover on the first day of the shift after a few at Wild Bill's Saloon in Banff the night before.

I had loaded the pack string in the corral under Johnny's critical eye. A few chiefs, subchiefs and assistant subchiefs from the warden service were also in attendance, getting their new government boots scuffed before they headed back to the office. Wasp was tied inside the corral just outside the barn.

I handed the lead rope from the pack horses to Joe and walked over to Wasp, picked up my reins and swung onto him. I quickly realized he was still tied to the corral. I must have looked pretty stupid. Before I could reach down and untie Wasp, Johnny, as I've said, a man of few words, gave me a disgusted look and shouted, "Untie your damn horse!"

Johnny taught me how to catch horses. At the Banff barn we would put out kibble and oats each morning in rubber containers inside the big corral or arena. Then Johnny would whistle and all 70 head would come swooping in through the open gate at a full gallop in a dusty confusion of flying hooves, biting and kicking to sort out who was going to feed with who and where. Once things settled down a little and the feed had been consumed, we would catch out our string.

Fired up, proud, wheeling this way and that, the morning sun glinting off them, they were a beautiful sight. But these oat-fired beasts didn't necessarily want to be caught. So how does a 90-kilogram human catch four wary, 500-kilogram horses out of 70 milling beasts?

Sometimes the prospects will stand and look at you while you simply walk up and put a halter on them without much fuss, but not always and not often. The larger the herd, the more complicated a pecking order you are about to interfere with.

A horse has two blind spots, one directly in front of it and the other directly behind. So if you walk into either when the horses are excited, there is a very good chance you will either be run over or kicked. You therefore approach them from a slight angle, moving slowly, hands down and relaxed, as if you just didn't care one way or another about catching them. That is non-threatening body language to a horse.

Horses are prey animals, and their flight at fright response is embedded deep in their conscious awareness.

Humans are predators. If you run or move quickly toward them with your hand up, "claws spread," and looking them straight in the eye, you can't blame them if they either just run over you or run away. You must keep your hands down when you approach a horse. When a horse did stand, Johnny would walk up and give it a pat or scratch on the chest as if to say, you can still run away before I put this halter on, it's your choice. The horse would stand while he slipped on the halter.

One morning two of us were trying to help Johnny catch a couple of wild ones by cornering them in the corral. This worked to begin with, but as soon as we took a step toward them they spooked and stampeded past us. We tried it again. When the moment came to move in on them Johnny shouted gruffly, "Keep your hands down and move slow but direct. Come up at an angle and don't look at him. Go up to him and catch him."

Once we did this the horses let us walk up and catch them. Johnny wasn't long on explanations about predator-prey relationships and all the horse whispering stuff that has since become so popular, but he did understand what made a horse stampede and what made him stand.

Sometimes the horses would get spooked up. Something might have happened at night—a cougar or wolf stalked them or the wind blew—but you knew by the nervousness of the herd that they were in a mood and that you had better be careful.

On one of those nervous mornings we were unable to catch a couple of the horses. Some of the herd charged around the corral, putting the other horses on edge. It was damn dangerous being in there and we were getting nowhere.

Johnny went into the barn and got a couple of catch ropes—three-metre pieces of ⅝-inch rope that were spliced back at both ends. They were used to slip around a horse's neck and move them without having to put a halter on. A band of about 20 horses charged toward Johnny at a gallop intent on running off or over somebody. He stood his ground in the middle of the arena. Suddenly he whipped the catch ropes down on the ground beside him a couple of times and shouted, "Get back!"

The horses skidded to a stop and stared at him. He slapped the ropes down smartly again, then walked up and caught the horse he wanted and led him away. Johnny had what some people call savvy. He intuitively knew what to do and when.

Old Style

Cal Hayes was what we called "old style." Ranch foreman at the Ya Ha Tinda, he had worked for the government and various ranches most of his life and had got his way most of the time. But like Johnny Nylund, if you saw past the bluff and bluster, there was a man you could learn from if you didn't close your mind.

Cal always wore one of those colourful cowboy bandanas wrapped tight around his throat, and the way I figured, that red silk bandana covered up his "red neck" for the most part.

When you stayed at the ranch, it became obvious that the cowboys who worked there had great respect for him and his old style, even if they didn't always agree.

At the end of a five-day horsemanship school at the ranch, Cal and I were walking down to the barns from the bunkhouse after a coffee break at the appointed hour (after all, it was a government ranch). We got talking about Wasp and Cal said, "That horse you are riding is proud, and you should be just as proud as he is when you're riding down the trail." Words to live by.

The horsemanship school was a wonderful idea. I had learned what I knew coming up through the school of hard knocks in the outfitting game. No one showed you anything and you learned by making mistakes or picking up the odd thing from somebody. When things didn't go well, you pushed harder. You also got hurt. But a horsemanship school—there was an idea and a chance to put a lot of things together, especially concerning safety.

Unlike the self-sufficient backcountry wardens described in Sid Marty's famous book *Men for the Mountains*, many of the new wardens were the prima donnas of the Parks Service. They didn't do hand work in the backcountry, they had their clothes and boots supplied down to their shorts, and each was assigned a new $3,000 Willow Creek saddle that sat in a locker in the barn except for use in the odd "Musical Ride." The trail crew picked their saddles from a bunch of old, ill-fitting saddles or provided their own. As with most of the equipment relating to our job, many items had to be acquired as hand-me-downs from the wardens.

The new-style wardens who actually went out on patrols would, for example, reluctantly make one cut in the middle of a log they couldn't ride around, then ride through, leaving the log to be cleared by the trail crew. You might gather that I didn't have a lot of respect for some of the "new-style" wardens. But I want to make it clear that there were also many hard-working and dedicated wardens who didn't hesitate to help out when the work was difficult. And they took calculated but big risks at times to save foolish people who got themselves in trouble in the mountains.

The early 1990s were a bad time for the warden service. Morale was fading fast and Ottawa bureaucrats were attacking the old esprit de corps that had produced so many savvy all-round wardens. By the late 1990s, morale reached an all-time low when the heritage minister suspended their enforcement authority.

The dedicated and able middle managers like my boss, Gord, eventually began to lose faith and quit trying to sway distant bureaucrats who marched to the tune of the latest management fad.

I recently ran into Gord at the funeral of a mutual friend, and he remarked, "It's worse now than when you were there.

Only thing to do is to find a place where you can feel like you are doing some good and stay there."

It took a lot of lobbying for the trail crew to be allowed to attend the horsemanship school. Training was seen as a perk for wardens and not something from which trail crew would benefit, even though I argued that we needed it most as we were always involved in horse-power–driven operations of one kind or another. In the end Joe and I did prevail (whined enough) and the trail crew was allowed to attend a couple of the horsemanship schools at the ranch.

The Ya Ha Tinda cowboys trained new colts every year and sent them out for the wardens and trail crew to use. The theory of the training program was that if we learned to ride the colts the way they'd been trained, everybody would get along much better. And that turned out to be true.

We started with basic ground handling, learned to tack up and bridle the colts the way they had been handled, and then practised riding under the watchful eyes of the Ya Ha Tinda trainers. The courses were centred on getting the job done with an approach that was safe for both horse and rider.

For example (recalling the morbid story about the hapless packer up north), it is a lot safer to face a restless pack string when you are mounting. The lead shank is draped forward toward the lead pack horse. You pick it up in your hand with the reins and mount. Once mounted, you are facing the anxious pack string and able to control them.

Aboard a horse like Wasp that worked off his front end

as nimble as a ballet dancer, there was no chance of the pack string getting past you or running up from behind and jamming the sharp corner of a pack box into your leg. I still practise this method unless I am on a steep narrow trail.

These days a course in horsemanship seems like a practical thing to do, but 20 years ago, if you were a male born out west, you were just supposed to know what to do, and the rest you'd learn in the school of hard knocks. (Any red-blooded western Canadian boy is supposed to be born knowing how to ride horses and how to navigate across the Arctic using a needle floating in a peanut butter jar lid!)

Some years ago I was riding a young mare named Sassy. She came with my bride, Yvonne. Neither of us had much "horse sense," as the saying goes. I was riding Sassy at a trot, way too far forward in the saddle and not taking into consideration potential hazards, when all of a sudden Sassy ran into a wall of mosquitoes. She darted to the right and I was thrown off the horse.

My foot hung up in an ill-fitting stirrup. Sassy bolted, dragging me behind. She kicked high with both rear feet catching me in the buttocks and lifting me like a rag doll up and out of the stirrup. I hung suspended for a moment before slamming into the ground with the wind knocked out of me. Yvonne, who had been riding behind me and witnessed this calamity, rushed up, dismounted, and while cradling my head in her arms asked urgently, "Are you okay? Can you hear me?"

"Yes," I answered as I slowly recognized where I was. After a while I managed to get up. Yvonne caught Sassy. I mounted and carefully walked her back to the ranch, dismounted and hobbled into the house, where I swallowed a handful of painkillers with whisky. Then I quietly went to bed for a month. Such ugly incidents can be prevented with some good training and an awareness of safe equipment.

I took to heart much of the "new way" of doing things taught by the Ya Ha Tinda cowboys and came away thinking that maybe I didn't know as much as I thought I did, and that I should reevaluate my approach to working with horses.

The old hard-knocks school of horsemanship is just that, and it's usually you getting knocked around. After all, if you start with the premise that you are outweighed by at least 500 kilograms, it should give you a clue that it's better to use your head to solve problems than to get pushy. Anger is generally brought on by frustration, and frustration by ignorance, and that's when you get into trouble. There's an old saying that "Impatience is the only sin."

Today I demand a lot less discipline from my horses, but seem to get more cooperation. You must be firm but fair. Horses have a deep, innate sense of fairness, which is why I enjoy them so much. They will accept and thrive on discipline, and they will learn a task quickly provided you know what you want them to do and can anticipate how horse and rider will get there. But if you are unfair or mean-spirited in your dealings with them, they will either take revenge or let you down in a moment of need, and you will likely get hurt.

Ya Don't Read Yer Horses

During the training school days, the ranch cowboys cajoled us into learning things they figured each of us needed to work on. We were all assessed during the five-day school and an open discussion of our strengths and weaknesses was promised at the end of the course.

In true cowboy fashion, these fellows were not long on analysis, but accurate and to the point. Kenny, the lead trainer, summed up my weakness by saying, "Ya don't read yer horses." I thought about this for some time and with only an inkling about its meaning, proceeded to forget the comment.

A few days later Joe and I headed for Sunshine Pack Out with our regular string of horses: Wasp, Quark, Tip, Dale and Tarzan. We parked our trailer off to one side of the paved Sunshine parking lot and proceeded to dress everybody up, fasten packs and throw diamonds. I usually brushed and saddled Wasp first and then stored him away a little off to one side so that when the pack string was ready I would be able to get the show moving up the trail without delay.

When the horses were ready to go and we'd done our last check to see what we had along and what might still be lying on the seat of the truck, I sauntered over to Wasp, untied him, put my foot in the stirrup and swung onto him. As I have noted, Wasp would buck as soon as we got going down the trail and he decided to have a poop. But Wasp also bucked at other surprising times and in other surprising ways.

Now I am sure that a good rodeo bucking-horse rider would probably do fine at these times, but I am the last to claim that I am a wild bronc rider. True, after being dumped a few times I had learned to ride Wasp out if he was moving forward, but when Wasp decided to really turn it up it was generally a short, sharp and frightening exhibition of how not to stay on a horse.

Wasp would crouch like a cat and then jump straight upward. You'd go up with him but come down just a little slower than him, the momentum of your ejection having kept you airborne. Wasp would hit the ground precisely where he had stood a moment before, crouch even lower and then catapult skyward again with such force that it was surprising even in the heat of contact.

Coming down just slightly slower than Wasp meant that he would have completed his crouch and be on his way back toward you and the hot sun while you were still heading down. If you were lucky enough to meet this rising trajectory squarely, the shock would be sufficient to erase the thought of sexual pleasures from your mind for at least two weeks.

This time, like a shaken rag doll just kicked in the groin, I rose with Wasp again and was flung high into the air above him, splayed out like a cat dropped from a barn loft, my arms and legs flailing wildly in mid-air. Then Wasp was gone. There was nothing between me and the paved parking lot. As I hung suspended by the glory of anti-gravity thrust, for a small, painless moment I remembered that it's not getting bucked off that hurts, it's hitting the ground.

Unlike a cat that always lands on its feet, I came down on the Sunshine parking lot flat on my back. There was a long silence as Joe slowly made his way over to my still body. Later, looking back, he commented that it looked a little like one of those Wile E. Coyote and Road Runner cartoons where Wile E. runs off a cliff and then falls and falls and hits so hard the ground cracks around him. Little squiggle lines rise up around him that represent unsettled dust and also signify that the coyote's fate is in question.

I slowly turned on my side, pulled myself up on my knees, then stood up. I took note that a carload of tourists had watched this stampede exhibition, and I remembered a story Johnny had impressed on me when I first hired on. A story about a government employee who had lost his temper and beat a horse and how the public had witnessed this incident. The public had complained to the chief park warden and the SPCA and there had been hell to pay, not to mention that a certain person lost his job. Keeping this in mind, I walked over to Wasp and gently led him off into the trees out of sight of the public and whaled on the end of his nose with my fist a couple of times while uttering low but meaningful expletives.

I then led Wasp back to the parking lot, got on, picked up the pack string lead rope, nodded to Joe, and we proceeded up to Brewster Cabin where I went to bed for three days. I slowly got moving by using my metal water bottle filled with boiling water for heat and ingesting my supply of painkillers.

During those three days I asked Joe how many jumps I had stayed on. He said three, maybe four. I came to think that was a very generous reply from a wonderful partner.

There are three kinds of injuries: Minor Injuries are the little bumps and aches and pains, Grand Injuries are the type I've just described, and Serious Injuries put you in the hospital. This particular Grand Injury did not qualify as a Serious Injury, but it hurt for about 18 months.

During the three days in bed at Brewster Cabin, I had time to ponder what Kenny had said up at the Ya Ha Tinda. His words, "Ya don't read yer horses," echoed through my Tylenol-fuelled dreams.

I got to thinking about the big muscle that lies lengthways along a horse's neck and that the form of that muscle can tell you quite lot about a horse's frame of mind. If it feels hard as iron and is bulging out, there's a good chance there's something on the equine mind besides oats, and your translocation might be a part of that. And just because his ears are ahead instead of laid back doesn't mean your demise is not on the agenda.

A few weeks later Johnny helped us truck up to Shark's Mountain Pack Out and there we proceeded to saddle and pack as usual. At the moment of truth, I could see Joe and Johnny watching me walk over to Wasp. I stroked my hand down that rock-hard hunk of flesh running along his neck. I noted his deceiving eye, gently untied him and quickly stepped back to watch. He went into that stunning crouch in a flash and proceeded to jump and careen and twist around the parking lot like he was possessed.

Wasp was a true government horse; he didn't like to go to work. He continued to buck for longer than usual, as if there being no rider to turf onto the hard, gravelled lot meant that at least he'd get that saddle off. We stared wide-eyed at Wasp's enthusiasm.

Then he quit and stood panting and staring at his drooping reins and lead shank. I walked over to him, picked up his reins and lead shank and led him back to the pack string. I checked the saddle cinch and bridle, tied my slicker behind the saddle, faced the pack string, swung over him, picked up the reins, called my usual "Wagons ho" and headed up the trail thinking, "Ya gotta read yer horses."

It was a bonus that Johnny was there to witness my progress. Who knows, maybe he figured I'd finally learned something—not that he'd ever say. Though a couple of weeks later he did have a new bridle for me.

I learned later that Cal had picked up Wasp out of Bargett's Rodeo stock. He was what they called at the ranch a "bought horse," rather than one raised there. Wasp came by his abilities and temper honestly. The lesson

I learned is that if you read your horse, that is, pay attention to the mood he's in, you have a better chance of changing it without getting hurt.

After three years of riding Wasp out in the morning, I decided I would teach him not to buck when the horse poop hit his hocks. I reckoned the reason he was so afraid of anything hitting his hocks was because he had been caught up in ropes or something when he was younger.

It took a couple of hours over two mornings. I ran a rope around his neck and belly and back. I stroked the back of his legs a little harder each time I brushed him out, and finally I ran the rope down and across those talented hocks. He slowly learned that the ropes meant nothing much. Wasp settled and never bucked again as we headed out.

The funny thing is, I came to regret teaching him not to buck. The mornings just weren't the same—maybe even a little disappointing.

CHAPTER

2

Help!

THERE ARE TWO KINDS OF FOOLS: those who make ill-fated plans and those who go along with them.

We unloaded the horses and pack mules at the trailhead for the West Fork of the St. Mary's River. The St. Mary's River flows east out of the Purcell Mountains, and the logging road along it ends about 70 kilometres west of Kimberley in southeastern British Columbia. After a long, rough, slow haul up the logging road in the stock truck, as well as time spent ferrying the truck 40 kilometres to another trailhead where we would end our trip, we were anxious to get up the trail as the day was wearing on. It was late June and this was our first backcountry patrol of the season.

Walter, a local rancher, had been hired as our packer

for the trip. While I was ferrying the stock truck, he had saddled and packed the horses, and when we returned he was patiently snoozing at the trailhead, his dog snuggled up against him, but alert.

I would ride Bobby, a good-looking, stout black quarter horse. I mounted and fell in at the back of the procession behind Walter, who was riding his favorite lead horse, Jack. The pack string consisted of two mules, Jake and Jenny, a horse named Hank, and my new boss, Will, riding a big, dapple grey horse named Silver.

Many of the trails in the Purcell Mountains are old out-fitting trails and routes. Often guides or local hunters leave the first half kilometre of trail uncut so that others cannot easily find their camps and hunting grounds. Walter picked a route through the boulders and alder and we followed, stumbling and dodging our way around bogs, blowdowns and rocks. After a short time and some scouting back and forth on foot, we found a rough trail leading up the West Fork valley.

The Purcell Wilderness Conservancy Park was a recent addition to the provincial park system and not much was known about the area, so we were making this patrol to do an "ocular" inventory and to discover just where trails and camps were located should we have to access the area for a rescue or an enforcement incident.

After about an hour and a half, we came on an old camp. As usual, there were tin cans, pieces of plastic, rusting utensils, a fallen-down tent frame and an ill-maintained barbed-wire drift fence. These old-style camps were common throughout the park, and as we encountered them we would burn what we could, then flatten the tin cans, rotting stoves, utensils and barbed wire and pack it out with us. The first five years I worked in the Purcells, much time was spent hauling garbage from old camps, and at least one or two pack horses would be loaded down with junk by the time the usual eight-day trip was completed.

I don't blame anyone for the condition of the old camps. It's just the way it was. People threw their garbage wherever was handy. Towns threw garbage over embankments and into rivers. Most rural residents had a gully somewhere they used as a dump. Many Canadian cities still dump garbage and untreated sewage in the ocean. Thankfully, we've changed our camping ethics and continue to change for the better, but it's amazing to think that only a generation ago garbage was a sign of affluence and civilization.

After another hour of beating our way up the rough trail, we reached a small meadow at the base of the headwall. We found a suitably level camp area; above us was a series of grassy meadows ideal for grazing the animals.

We quickly unpacked and stripped the saddles from the horses and pack mules. Then we hobbled the stock and turned them out for a well-deserved feed of lush alpine grass. Hobbling basically means you put a pair of leather or chain "handcuffs" on the front feet of the animals and turn them loose. This leaves them free to graze, but discourages them from heading down the trail. We set up our tents and spread out our sleeping bags and mattresses. We dug out a small round of sod and made our fire there. We'd later replace the sod so there'd be little trace of the camp. Will was big on no-trace camping, and rightly so. As it had been a long day of trucking up from the Columbia Valley to the trailhead, followed by considerable bushwhacking, trail finding and trail cutting, we ate supper and were quickly asleep.

Early next morning Walter's dog, Help, a two-year-old female border collie, was missing. She had started up the trail with us, but in our deliberations through blowdowns, bogs and boulders, she had not come along. It was decided that Walter would go back down the valley to look for her while Will and I stayed and scouted the trail ahead toward the pass. Walter saddled Jack and headed down, backtracking the way we had come.

During the day, Will and I scouted some game trails and hiked down to the old camp to roll up some more wire we had seen lying in the bush. We didn't have room to take it along this time so we hung up the roll so it would be easily found next time we passed by.

Walter eventually returned with Help following along behind. He had found her at the trailhead overlooking the valley, sitting where she and Walter had waited for us the previous day.

As the day had now worn on and the climb up the head-wall would take us into unknown territory, we decided to wait till next morning to continue the journey. We settled into our camp for a slow evening. The horses and mules were grazing contentedly, and Help and Walter were reunited.

Will studied his map and indicated that we were going over the pass to the southwest, about 600 metres higher. Patches of snow still covered the summit and I worried aloud that the north and west sides would have a lot more snow since it was early in the season. But Will pointed to dots on the map showing a route over and around a basin on the other side. He was intent on his mission to check out some old outfitter camps in Billy Goat Basin to see if they had indeed been cleaned up. Will stared at his map.

I had guided in the mountains for 13 years before joining the Parks Service as a ranger. And about 10 years ago I had spent a fall season working out of the same camp as Walter, guiding hunters on the Spillimacheen River. I asked him if he was still guiding up there.

"No," he answered slowly.

I noted hesitation in his voice and after another moment or two of campfire meditation asked, "So why did you quit the Spillimacheen, Walter?"

"I kinda got my feelings hurt."

"Did you have a bad hunter?"

"No, the hunter was real good," Walter paused.

"You didn't get paid?"

"No, it wasn't that. Something happened on a bear hunt that hurt my feelings."

Silence. I waited.

"Those grizzlies are different."

Another long silence.

"What do you mean, Walter?" It was clear I would have to dig a bit to get Walter's story.

"We were on a spring bear hunt and things just didn't go that well between the outfitter and me. His wife was mad 'cause I had taken a hunter for a two-day campout and they had seen a couple of bears where they were. Anyway, we settled all that and then next day we went to look for the bears.

"It didn't take long to find them, on a snowslide not far from the base camp; two good-sized grizzlies, both males. I got my hunter, lined up on one of them and he shot. The bear went down right there. But the other one didn't run off."

Walter stopped. He was obviously upset, remembering the incident. It couldn't have been just the bear being shot that was bothering Walter. He was a pioneer, rancher and hunter and familiar with the fate of animals. I fed our little campfire some fuel.

"The other bear just stayed there, and then it picked the dead bear up in its arms and held it to its chest, just like a man. It was standing out there on the snowslide, on its hind legs, and holding its wounded brother and wouldn't let go. Then it started bawling." Walter's voiced faltered and by the campfire light I could see that he was tearful.

"Jesus!" I exclaimed. "What happened then?"

"Well, I had to go up there and chase the bear off so the hunter could get his trophy. And the outfitter was spooked so he wouldn't back me up. So I had to go up alone and chase that bear off. He hung onto the dead bear, just like a man."

Will and I were silent. Embarrassed, I guess, to see Walter so moved. I told a story about caribou hunting up north and how they would run up to you and stand there and watch you butcher their kin. How I had to chase off the caribou witnesses.

It helped to heal the moment.

Walter wandered off to get some brush for the morning fire and to check his horses. Will and I watched the fire burn down and then turned in.

The next day was clear and sunny. We packed up our camp quickly and headed up the steep headwall. Most mountain valleys become steeper and steeper as one nears their source. Often streams start in these large basins that gather much snow during the winter and then slowly release their water over the summer and fall as the snow melts. The West Fork of the St. Mary's was a typical, large alpine basin with a series of steep pitches leading to a ridge.

We climbed steadily, leading the horses and following elk and goat paths till we were about 450 vertical metres above our camp. We stopped and rested and looked down the valley from where we had come. We could see Help far below us, heading for the previous night's camp. Walter went back again.

After he returned, we began traversing the last 150 metres of climb. This involved crossing a fairly steep snow patch, and midway across the snow, Jake, the mule, fell and slid. Fortunately, the snow patch levelled at the bottom and he came to a sliding halt without any injuries or damage to the equipment.

We waited while Walter again went back and brought Jake up to the last bunch of larch trees. Finally we were all gathered at treeline: Walter and Help, Will and myself; Jack, Silver, Hank and Bobby, the horses; and Jake and Jenny, the mules. We traversed the last pitch of climb on snow patches and reached the summit.

We had a spectacular, panoramic view of mountains and snowfields. To the north lay the granite ridges of St. Mary's Alpine Park, to the west the divide into the West Kootenay, and behind and far below, the valley we'd come from.

I peered down the even steeper headwall on the west side. A huge cornice extended out over the ridge and there seemed to be no place to get through with the pack animals. At a point where the snow cornice was the narrowest I suggested to Walter that maybe we could cut a trail through the cornice and traverse across the first snow patch and get around onto firmer ground.

Will was anxious to go down into Billy Goat Basin and check out the outfitters' camps and quickly agreed. Walter said he didn't like travelling on the snow since Jake had already lost his footing and slid down some ways before stopping in a gully of snow.

The old snow on the west side of the mountain was packed hard by the wind and sun, and even the mule's small feet only sank in a few centimetres. The trick was to angle across the snow slope and stay away from the boulders popping up through the snow pack. The rocks absorbed heat and the snow around them was rotten—a good place to break a leg or have a horse trapped in a three-metre-deep hole.

I took out my saddle axe and began cutting a notch in the snow cornice and tramping a narrow trail. After about a half hour of work, I had a trail made through the cornice and across the snow slope to a bare patch of ground.

There was no doubt in my mind that we were taking a chance, but this was the first trip with my new boss; he wanted to go down into the basin, and I foolishly underestimated our route. We had left no backup vehicle at the West Fork trailhead where we started, and going back would mean a long 40-kilometre ride on the road. We decided to find our way down the slope into Billy Goat Basin.

I led Bobby into the notch. The trusting four-year-old plunged in up to his belly, floundered, then got to his feet and carefully followed me as I kicked steps across the exposed snow slope.

We reached a bare patch of ground on the far side of the snow, and I motioned for Will to proceed. He stepped on the snow slope and fell. I watched through the viewfinder of my camera in disbelief as he accelerated down the snow slope in a sitting position and made no effort to arrest his fall. He bounced across a pile of rocks on his rear and came to a jarring halt just short of a 150-metre drop. Slowly he got up and traversed toward me onto the dry ground.

When he reached me I took note of his smooth boots, some scratches and scrapes, and a very frightened look on his face. It dawned on me that Will, who had planned this trip, was a novice in mountain terrain.

Silver stood waiting where Will had fallen, and behind him waited Walter, his horse, and the pack string. I did not want to take Bobby back across the slope, nor did I particularly want to cross it again myself, but now it seemed we were fully committed. I handed Bobby's lead rope to Will and headed back across the snow slope to where Silver waited.

I made five more trips, each time with another animal and each time praying that they would not slip, give me a push, or worse, fall on me and take us both down the slope and into the rocks below. Each animal had to be coaxed and cajoled to take the first step through the cornice, where they plunged into soft snow to their bellies and then had to flounder up onto the harder snow—something foolish they would never do unless a human talked them into it.

At last we were all safe on the bare patch. Safe, but surrounded by steep snow slopes and goat terrain and no way back. Walter didn't fancy going on the snow slopes again, so

I scouted some steep, short, bare benches and narrow ledges. It looked like it would go. I climbed back up to the waiting pilgrims and asked, "Which way, Walter, snow or rock?"

"Rocks." He nodded toward the steep slopes.

Slowly and carefully we made our way down, eventually coming to what would be the crux of our journey—a narrow and exposed rock ledge that the already bewildered animals would have to traverse, followed by a half-metre jump up onto another ledge. A mistake would mean falling hundreds of metres onto the jagged rock below. Once through the step, though, it looked clear and easy. I led out along the ledge and asked Bobby to make the jump. In a second he was up beside me. I took him along a much wider ledge to a reasonable slope where one lonely alpine fir stood and tied him to it.

I looked back to see Will trying to bring Silver through the narrow jump. Will was standing in front of Silver and pulling on the lead shank. Silver was getting more and more excited. I hurried back and moved Will out of the way as I reached for the lead shank. I stood aside and asked Silver to try, and again he flailed at the jump. By now he was quite agitated. I decided that I had to turn him around and try to find another way down. Before I could move, he made another desperate try at the step, rearing up as he again balked.

The lead shank slipped from my hand like a caress as Silver lost his balance and began to go over backward. He looked at me as if to say, "I'm trying as hard as I can." And then he disappeared, cartwheeling down the jagged cliff below, striking rocks and bouncing onto a steep snow slope. He smashed against a pile of rocks and carried on down till he finally came to rest on a rocky bench. A loud red scar followed him down the slope.

We stared down the cliff. Silver gave a couple of kicks and lay still. The bright, hot sun beat in on us. How long we stood there and watched in disbelief I don't know. But eventually I found myself leading Bobby down toward the lifeless form on the snow. Walter and Will took the other animals back along another ledge and managed to get into a dish-shaped snow slope and down to where Silver lay without further mishap. Walter reached Silver and pulled the busted tack off him.

"I am sorry, Walter, I am sorry," I said.

"Some will say it's a big joke. I think we should say nothin'. We'll just carry on," said Walter.

We quietly repacked the broken gear and started down again. Silver was left for the bears, eagles and ravens. We reached tree line and scouted a game trail through a wood-choked gully to a small meadow. Exhausted, we unpacked, turned out the animals and made camp.

I felt responsible for what had happened up there. The worst of it was that look in the horse's eyes before he went over. Still trusting. I figured I knew something about working in the mountains with horses. I didn't know anything! I was disgusted with myself.

Help!

I set to work cooking supper. I didn't want to face Walter. He and Will rested. I could see them talking quietly. After a while Walter went down and filled his water bottle by the creek. He came over to where I was sitting by the fire, looked at me and offered me the water.

I think that was the sweetest water I ever drank.

In all the confusion, Help had disappeared back over the mountain. No dog, a dead horse, a foolish plan. Maybe Help knew better; she'd wanted nothing to do with it from the start.

We found her three days later, hungry but well, again sitting where she and Walter had sat looking over the valley, waiting for the trip to begin.

3

Reid Goes Natural

YESTERDAY YVONNE AND I DROVE to the Royal Antler Ranch to see how our geldings pastured there were doing. Reid, the ranch foreman, greeted us as we arrived and promptly invited us into the house for a beer.

We made our way to the house and settled into a couple of comfortable old armchairs to discuss the matters of the day. Reid had just acquired a new dog, so dog stories were in order.

"We had a dog one time that was a bit messed up. I guess it had been a top sled dog up at Atlin, but the fellow who owned it had driven him too hard and broke his spirit. This made the dog overly timid, which was not his true nature as he was part wolf.

"The incident I'm going to relate happened when we worked at the Boundary Ranger Station at Kananaskis Park. We lived there for about four years.

"There are a lot of coyotes out there and they were a pretty friendly lot. In fact, they would form a pack at night right at the back of the house and howl. This was fun at first, but the constant howling kept everybody awake. The coyotes were a nuisance. And Ole Dan, the half-wild, retired Atlin sled dog, would join the party and bark his lungs out half the night.

"One night I conceived of a plan to play a trick on these coyotes and be rid of them for good. My plan had a sinister, fail-proof ecological reasoning behind it.

"After dark, when the coyotes had gotten in full swing and Ole Dan had joined in from the edge of the lawn, doing his best to fulfill whatever part of him was still wolf, I would sneak out of bed, then out of the house and around behind the pack of howling coyotes. I would jump out of the bush like a madman, growling and screeching at the top of my lungs and land right in the middle of the pack. To add to the effect, I would be stark naked! If wild was what they wanted, I would give them a real charge. They would be so scared they would never howl again, let alone near the house.

"A few days later, about 10 minutes after midnight on a full moon night, the commotion of barking and howling canines had reached a feverish pitch. I crept out of the house and into the woods behind the pack. The coyotes and Ole Dan were in a howling trance. Suddenly, without the slightest warning, I pounced, stark naked, from out of the trees and into the centre of the circle of howling coyotes, yelling and screaming like a banshee ghost.

"For a long moment the coyotes froze where they sat, unable to fathom this appearance. The screeching apparition stunned them. Had they conjured up this hairless beast or was it the moon's sad reflection?

"With the quick wisdom of their breed, they snatched quick looks at their brothers and sisters and instantly knew this was some fool human out of control. They vanished into the thick timber.

"Ole Dan was not as steady of nerve. Having had to deal with one crazy human master already, he took one look at this show and headed off at full speed out of the yard and down the road as hard as his old sled-dog legs could carry him. We did not see him for about a week until, quite by accident one day, I found him cowering under the front porch.

"Poor Dan never did seem the same after that terrible night when his master went natural. As for the coyotes, they were back the next night, howling and yipping as usual."

CHAPTER

4

Living the Life

WORKING AS A BACKCOUNTRY RANGER in the Purcell
Wilderness Conservancy Park, I patrol this protected area
on horseback.

During the patrol season my wrangler and I typically
make backcountry patrols of four to nine days in duration.
The length of time of the patrols depends on weather, time
of year, intuition and local information as to the whereabouts of visitors and commercial operators.

The backcountry day starts at dawn, when we catch and
bring the horses in from the grazing areas. They are each fed
a coffee can of high-protein feed. Mark, my wrangler, usually
makes breakfast. We eat, lingering over our coffee, then take
down and pack up the camp, and saddle and pack the stock.

From the time we start breaking camp till we swing into the saddle is two hours of steady work. Then we ride for six or seven hours, sometimes longer, to the next camp.

Along the way I check on the amount of use grazing areas have had, interview travellers, check the condition of camps, note wildlife sightings, cut trail and observe the area for natural changes or human impacts. Sometimes I collect data for specific studies.

We usually reach our destination by late afternoon. We unpack, put up the tent, lay bedding out to dry, set the stove, unsaddle the horses and store the tack on a pole under a tarp, cut firewood, wash, cook supper, do the dishes, take the horses to a grazing area, hobble them, make notes on the day, check the horses again and sleep.

People often comment that I must have lots of time for writing when I am in the bush, but the exact opposite is true. Travelling in the backcountry, we are in the saddle day after day for seven or eight hours and making new camps every night, which doesn't leave much free time. The weather any season of the year can be rain, sun, snow, wind, heat, cold, mud, high rivers or calm, pristine alpine days.

Darn Bells

I have become accustomed to hearing horse bells at night. If I don't hear horse bells I can't sleep. I wake up and listen awhile and usually hear a tinkling sound brought on the night wind, but if I don't hear a bell I get up, throw on some clothes and go out and check to see if our transportation is still in the vicinity. When the horses have had a good feed and their bellies are full, they stand still for a long time.

My horses are good about staying around and have come to know the camps and grazing areas we usually stay in. They've also figured out that home and the morning feed of kibble is where the tent is.

Most mornings they come in on their own just before dawn. George, my lead horse, a tall, well-built saddlebred–quarter horse, has been with me for nine years. He has the largest bell. Usually he comes into camp nosing around for feed just before dawn, and not finding it handy, stands by the tent swinging his head from side to side, clanging his darn bell till I get up and make breakfast.

Horses thrive on routine and they get used to certain areas. Joe M, an old-time guide, told me a story about a hunter he was guiding on Toby Creek. Joe was a logger and truck driver for many years, but in the early 1980s, when he turned 50, he just dropped out and started making homemade buckskin clothing, living in a tent and generally spending as much time in the backcountry as possible— Joe's solution to his mid-life crisis.

The back end of Toby Creek is two days' ride from a main road. The hunter Joe was guiding was from a large city in the States, and as Joe told it, this fellow was terrified and fixated on the idea that they might be lost and left to the bears in the high country.

It was Joe's habit to leave camp early in the morning before light and ride to a lookout. He would spend part of the day there glassing for game. Around noon he'd turn his horses loose for an hour so they could graze. The American hunter was adamant that Joe should not do this. He was scared stiff that the horses would run away and that he and Joe would be stranded.

He insisted vehemently that Joe hang onto the reins of the horse while it fed. Finally Joe asked, "Just where do you think the horse is going to run to if I let him go?"

"Well he might run home and leave us to the bears!" the jittery American answered.

"Home?" asked Joe. "This is his home!"

A Vile Concoction

One summer we participated in a grizzly bear DNA sampling project. Hair traps, consisting of a strand of barbed wire temporarily nailed to a tree about knee height and encircling about 100 square metres, had been set at various locations throughout the park. Inside each trap, a vile concoction of rotted fish and blood that had stood in a drum in the sun for a month was poured onto a pile of debris. The stink attracts the bears, but does not reward them. For some reason, bears will not climb over the wire, but instead crawl underneath. In so doing they leave hair with follicles attached caught in the barbs. These samples are collected and sent to a lab for analysis. DNA sampling reveals the kinship among bears, while other tests provide interesting information about the bear's recent diet. Such information helps compare the lineage of bears from adjoining areas and regions so that genetic "corridors" critical to maintaining healthy populations can be identified.

Our job was to collect the hair samples every 10 days for 40 days and bait the traps with the vile concoction. Mike, our resource officer, and I had a good summer collecting samples. On one occasion, however, we could not reach the upper part of Findlay Creek by horse because the rivers were in full runoff and too dangerous to cross.

We brought in a helicopter to ferry us and our bait to a couple of the traps in the upper reaches of Findlay Creek. It was a hot summer day. We had been successfully packing the bait in two-litre pop bottles in the bottom of a pack box. And though the horses were upset when they got scent of the stuff, we had not had any incidents beyond some general excitement. The bait was so vile that a whiff of the scent caused me to vomit.

Mike stowed the bottles in the trunk of the helicopter and we flew to the trap site. After landing he took the bottles to the trap. He unscrewed the cap on one of the bottles, and to his dismay the concoction sprayed out in a blast, covering him in a heavy mist of rotted fish and blood. The liquid had been super-vibrated and pressurized in the helicopter.

John, the helicopter pilot, and I were fortunate to be out of range, but Mike stunk so badly we would only allow him in the cabin of the helicopter without his clothes, which were then stored in the trunk, and only after he had a cold bath in the creek. He still reeked of the stuff, and we flew back with the windows open.

Enforce the Law or Move on

As a park ranger, some days I enforce the law, usually the Wildlife Act, Liquor Act or Park Act and Regulations, and that can mean confrontation. You take an oath that you will enforce the law. It is "the job" and we are told we don't have a choice about this.

"If you don't want to enforce the law then move on."

Consequently, it seems that often when I visit with the public or a commercial operator, it is guaranteed they will either resent your presence or at the least have a long complaint about someone in the Parks Service or the Parks Service in general. After all, who wants a park ranger around when you're living out a fantasy about the good ole days when you could do whatever you felt like? The backcountry tends to attract the more independent types.

Park rangers are peace officers, but though I carry a rifle in the backcountry, we do not carry side arms as conservation officers or the RCMP do. Not carrying side arms is a mixed blessing. We often check hunters who are carrying firearms and it seems that because we do not wear a side arm our enforcement authority is not recognized or respected.

Last year in the backcountry, I encountered a hunter

who was so threatening and resentful of authority that it gave me cause to wonder if in some situations we should be armed. On the positive side, we generally handle such situations at a so-called PR level, and should something more serious develop, reinforcements are brought in. In any case, a peace officer must not approach a dangerous situation alone, and who would? Sometimes, though, the danger of the situation is not evident till you're in it.

Hot Days, Cool Thoughts

I usually eat lunch out of my saddlebag while travelling, but on hot days, for a break from the heat, I tie the horses under the shade of giant pines or spruce near creeks where cool winds blow down. Then I crawl into the shade of the creek bank and stay there for an hour sipping water, letting my body temperature cool and giving the horses a rest.

When you are still for a while you see more wildlife. They are generally watching you if you are moving and become still, fading into the background until you have passed.

Hunkered down along a creek, I've observed a water ouzel or western sandpiper work the rocky creek banks for insects. Western sandpipers will land at the beginning of a strip of exposed rocky shoreline and carefully work their way along it, picking up stoneflies, then turn and just as carefully rework their path to their starting point before flying away.

Watching them feed raises questions about how many kilometres of boulder-strewn, mountain stream bank it takes to support a pair of sandpipers. When we build a bridge, do we take into consideration that rocky creek banks support the insects these birds feed on? Maybe another location would work?

If the weather is so bad that I shouldn't travel, which only happens a day or two a year, I stay in camp and wait it out. I catch up on my sleep and paperwork.

As we travel I read sign: tracks, turned stones, torn logs, chewed brush. I want to know what or who is ahead of me. I watch the country, making mental notes of changes, and I watch the horses. Their senses are keener than mine and they communicate a steady patter of information about where we are and who or what else is around.

The business of travel, awareness and observation fills the day to brimming.

CHAPTER

5

A Sharp Knife

RALPH JOHNSEN IS FROM MY home community in Alberta and works as a helicopter engineer. Helicopters require daily maintenance, and an engineer is stationed with the aircraft wherever it is working. His work often took him to remote wilderness areas, and Ralph eventually based himself out of the small mining and tourism community of Atlin, in British Columbia's northwest corner.

Some called Atlin "Switzerland of the North." Situated on the east side of Atlin Lake and just east of Canada's spectacular Coast Mountain Range, this old gold-rush town is home to a handful of winter souls and many tourists, guides and miners during the summer. Most of Ralph's helicopter work came during the busy summer exploration and outfitting season, so during the winter he sold and re-paired snowmobiles and small engines.

He was also a very talented knife-maker; his knives were highly prized for their beauty and function, and I owned one of these knives. A Johnsen knife is well balanced, the handle large and made to fit one's hand, and the blade has a drop point like fingers. As you use it, you know where the tip is because it feels like an extension of your hand.

During the mid-1980s, I worked in the Bonnet Plume Territory near the Arctic Circle, guiding hunters in a vast and incredibly beautiful northern world rich in wildlife and weather. As the winter season closed in, I headed south on the Alaska Highway toward my home in southeastern British Columbia. It is a 36-hour drive from Whitehorse to Radium Hot Springs. It would take a couple of days, and since an extra day would make little difference to my schedule, I decided to swing down to Atlin and visit Ralph.

I asked around town and was soon directed to his home-based shop. Aside from seeing my old friend, there was also a business reason for visiting. To a guide and northern wil-derness traveller, a knife is the most useful of tools—carried with you always and kept sharp. I had purchased a Johnsen knife a year ago, but had a difficult time putting a keen edge on the very hard, high-quality steel. Stainless steel knives can be challenging to sharpen until you have the knack of "finding" the edge.

I was not about to blame the knife for not having a keen

edge. But I reckoned that if I visited the knife's maker I would surely learn the art of sharpening.

Seeking a lesson, I entered Ralph's dark bear's den of a repair shop, and there in the dim light I saw his stout, solid figure bent over some work at his bench.

After some preliminary greetings I got the feeling that as much as Ralph would like to visit, he was also in the middle of a project and therefore anxious that I should state my business. The fact that I had not seen him for a couple of years mattered little to Ralph. Like many involved craftsmen, he lived in the present, and the present was demanding his time.

I brought my knife out of its snug sheath and explained that I couldn't seem to get an edge on it, being sure to intimate that it was not the knife at fault but my own shortcoming as a sharpener of knives.

Ralph, backlit from his bench light, lifted his head from the workbench, and his eyes glared out of the darkness like smouldering welding rods. There was a long silence.

I explained again that I clearly understood the knife was not at fault and that what I sought was a sharpening lesson from an expert. After further consolidating my position by grovelling and eating even larger pieces of humble pie, Ralph agreed to teach me how to sharpen a knife.

"Start with a carborundum block, and slice the knife's shoulder away until a precise and even angle can be accessed with a diamond-coated steel stick or porcelain rod. These knives are hollow ground. The blade is concave and gives you access to a very fine angle for sharpening the edge."

Sounds simple enough, but as I had learned, the technique of sharpening custom-made knives, and even information about knife sharpening, can be difficult to acquire.

A few years later, I visited Ralph at our home community of Spruce View, Alberta, where he was working with his brother on their family farm. Ralph, when not distracted from his work by pilgrims seeking knowledge, loves to sit back and discuss affairs of state and takes a philosophical approach to most questions, that is except knife sharpening. He is also an inventor; he loves to improve on the tried and true and had manufactured a gleaming hoof pick that he was anxious to have tested.

Hoof picks are essential tools to horsemen. This hand-sized tool is used not only to clean a horse's hoof to prepare it for shoeing, but also for prying rocks loose that lodge between the iron shoe and pocket of the hoof, and for other general hoof maintenance. Packed in a saddlebag or in a case on one's belt, this pocket knife–sized tool is usually plain and inexpensive.

All too often one is given a hand tool with a handle that is too small or thin, unbalanced or ugly, or with the wrong angle for the work the tool is supposed to do. One of the advancements Ralph has brought to hand tools is the care with which he shapes the handles. They fit in your hand and are an extension of the fingers; they are balanced, functional and attractive.

A characteristic of doing business with Ralph's family is that the customer must be satisfied before they make their payment: be it a cow, hay or hoof pick.

I have heard it said by less scrupulous people that a guarantee is the cheapest thing you can give. But with Ralph, his word is guarantee and bond. And contrary to the impression given in the "bad news" media, a lot of businesses still operate this way. If they didn't, I think our whole system would crash.

So it was that I took a hoof pick on trial. I tried it out and used it from time to time. The one criticism I have of this tool is that it is too beautiful for its utilitarian purpose, and it was therefore squirrelled away in a cupboard rather than put to work on a daily basis. The deal I made with Ralph was that the next time I was passing through I could either return the pick or pay for it. Price to be negotiated at that time. Both of us knew that there was often a couple of years or more between visits.

Time has a way of passing without notice, and somehow I didn't pass through Ralph's town for more than a few years. From time to time I felt guilty that I had not settled my debt, but every time I was headed to Alberta I was in a hurry and didn't plan the time to visit and close the deal.

A few more years went by. The hoof pick stayed in the

cupboard, not so much because I didn't want to use it, but because I had no right to use it.

It is interesting the way one rationalizes and forgets these things. Once in a while I would run across the hoof pick and be reminded that I needed to pay Ralph or return the pick. But then I wasn't really using it, and it did turn out to be too fancy for its intended use, and I debated if I could really afford a $100 hoof pick. And so I would leave it until I could visit Ralph and discuss the matter.

By the time five years had gone by, I felt so guilty about not settling the matter that I was embarrassed to bring it up and now avoided the situation on that account.

I remember as a young boy asking my father what the most valuable thing in the world was. He would look down with his mystical grey-blue eyes, pause for a moment and say, "Peace of mind, son, peace of mind."

There would be no peace of mind till I had either paid for the darn hoof pick or returned it.

I decided to immediately send Ralph a cheque for $100 with a note saying I was sorry to be late getting back to him, but better late than never. I took the envelope down to the post office and posted the cheque with a great sense of relief.

About two weeks later the letter came back marked "wrong address, return to sender."

About a year passed. Ralph's brother John was vacationing at their timeshare at a local resort. John and I had gone through grade school together. Wendy, John's wife, called and invited us for a dinner. I decided that now was the time to settle this hoof pick thing. I wrote another cheque with a note, took it to the dinner and gave it to John with instructions to deliver it to Ralph. He said I really should go and visit Ralph and deliver the cheque. I said I'd put this thing off long enough, and every time I had been going to settle the matter something had come up. I had gone from guilt to embarrassment to remorse and enough was enough!

Since that time I have taken possession of probably the finest hoof pick ever made and have been carrying it in the truck and on my horse and feeling good about using it, even if it is too fancy. It is, as a friend once said of a fine tool, "A thing of beauty and joy forever."

About three months after I sent the cheque, I received a letter from Ralph acknowledging that he had cashed the cheque and had up until that time forgotten about the hoof pick, but was glad I had remembered. He also expressed a fine sentiment about our parents raising us right and told me that I owed him a visit.

CHAPTER

6

The More Time
I Spend with Horses

RICK, A WRANGLER WHO WAS making a trip with me into the Purcells, observed, "The more time I spend with horses the less I like people."

Rick is a dropout. He had lived in cities most of his life and worked as an ironworker building steel structures. During his time off, he would travel with his horses and hunt in the wilderness country of British Columbia.

I had no trouble agreeing with Rick. Most horses are honest. If you treat them fairly they work their hearts out for you; if you are mean, they become mean. I have since related this quote to people and to my surprise found that some were insulted by it—usually those who had not had the privilege of working with these wonderful animals.

I thought for some time about why people were insulted by this comparison and speculated it has to do with an arrogance that shuns other species.

How could it be possible a horse's company might be preferable to theirs? How could it be possible that time spent with another species could teach us about ourselves? Are human lives not de facto more important than animal lives?

I considered these questions as I drove back from a visit to Toby Creek trailhead. I had checked the register there and made some repairs to the trailhead signs. As I sped down the Toby Creek road and then slowed for a narrow curve cut into a rock bluff above the river, a large, tawny cat suddenly dashed across the road and disappeared into the open forest above me.

It's very unusual to see a mountain lion or cougar in broad daylight. In 25 years travelling in the wilderness I had only seen one other. Cats are nocturnal hunters and reclusive, seldom seen.

I pulled the truck over to the side of the road and shut off the engine. I opened the door, got out, flipped the seat forward, took my 12-gauge Defender out of its scabbard and slipped a few slugs into the magazine. I figured I'd wander up into the forest and see if I might get another glimpse of the cat. I had no intention of shooting it, but to be on the safe side should things turn, at least I could make some noise.

I scrambled up the embankment and peered into the bush. Nothing. I walked slowly toward a small opening and crossed it. When I reached the other side of a small meadow I stopped, squatted and peered intently into the surrounding pine and poplar forest. I saw the cougar. It was about 60 metres away, a big, healthy animal, a good 2 metres long including the tail and weighing about 70 kilograms. It met my stare unflinchingly and had been watching me.

As our eyes met, the cat crouched and then started to move toward me in a slow, stalking posture like a house cat hunting a mouse. I checked my gun to be sure it was loaded and looked around nervously.

Just above me was a small cliff about three metres high; a perfect launching place for a predator. I quickly decided that the best place to be was back across the small opening and away from the rock ledge. I backed up slowly as the cat continued to move steadily toward me.

Feeling in control of the situation, I thought this would be a good time to test the advice we routinely give the public regarding cougar attacks. The literature says that if a cat is stalking you, you should wave your arms in the air. I did this. I moved my arms above my head and waved them; the cat immediately crouched lower and became more intent on its prey.

Prey? Well yes, I guess I was its prey! Realizing that this predator was intent on attacking and possibly eating me, my arrogance and feeling of being in control vanished. I felt cold fear trickle down my spine. This was more serious than I had expected. I regretted being quite so cocky about waving my arms.

But reason kicked in. I flicked the safety on the gun to the fire position, again checked the chamber to be sure it was loaded and brought the sighted shotgun to my shoulder. I was grateful I had practised at the shooting range earlier that week. I was also darn glad I was not standing here trying to fish out my Swiss Army knife.

The cougar began to move more quickly across the forest floor; silently and deliberately it was closing the gap between us. It was now only 12 metres away. It glared and showed its teeth. I remembered what a crusty old conservation officer who gave us a bear-spray course told me, "Once animals are goal-oriented the spray won't work."

I took aim at the cat. Strangely, I felt fear turn into indignant anger. "Who the hell do you think you are? You don't attack humans!" I heard myself say. I could shoot the cat. But there was no need for that.

The cougar sprang into the opening. I fired a slug about 10 centimetres in front of the cat's outreached paw and jacked another shell into the chamber. But before the deafening blast had stilled, the cat was gone.

I slowly lowered the shotgun and peered into the empty clearing. I backed carefully toward the truck. My heart was pounding. The sharp focus of adrenaline had kicked in. Every step I took crackled, and I realized I was totally aware of my surroundings down to the minutest detail. My vision was crisp, my hearing tuned.

At the truck I unloaded the shotgun and stowed it back in the scabbard behind the seat. I sat in the cab for a moment, remembering the lithe figure of the cougar as it sprang into the opening and the dirt flaring up in its face as I fired.

That was close enough. And so much for waving my arms in the air—maybe the cat thought they were antlers. The other advice we give is to holler and get a stick or a rock or whatever you can grab, and fight for your life. This still seemed appropriate. But I was glad I had chosen to bring the gun.

Someone said the definition of wilderness was a place where you can get eaten. It is also a place where nature humbles us, a place where we humans are not in control, a place where feelings and reactions that have been dormant for a long time are intensely evoked.

I started the truck and continued down the Toby Creek road. I thought about how quickly my arrogance had turned to fear, and strangely, how at the critical moment it had turned to focused and indignant anger—the clarity of anger when threatened.

My anger was driven by insult, by the fact that an animal would dare to attack me, a human! There was that arrogance again that I had so carefully buried and rationalized—the arrogance of assumed control over nature.

CHAPTER

7

Ox's Clothesline

AS PART OF MY MARRIAGE endowment I received a thoroughbred mare, but we were in a bind for a place to board her. Our place was not fenced yet so we approached our neighbour, Ox, about keeping Sassy at his farm on the nearby reserve. Ox had always been friendly, and we were pleased when he agreed to rent us a pasture.

One fine spring day I found myself driving down Shuswap Creek road to Ox's to check on the mare. I parked near his house, stepped out of my truck and took in the situation before me.

It didn't take long to see that Ox was having a bad time getting his newly built clothesline to work. I observed that the line had come off the roller at the far end of his rigging. Normally this would not have caused Ox much consternation, but since he had had a double hernia operation the previous fall and was 63 years of age, he was contemplating whether or not he should climb up the tree again at the far end of the line and fix it. His gut was already sore from a full day's exertion.

I could see that Ox had limbed his spar tree from the ground up to where the line was attached, leaving climbing stumps the full length of the trunk. At the lower end of the rigging was a platform about two and a half metres off the ground, precariously perched alongside the roof of his carport. Here the base end of the line was attached to a stout anchor pole.

The thing that made this whole outfit so impressive was that this clothesline rig was long enough to hold the entire wardrobe of Ox's spouse, five children and the dozen or so foster kids who were nearly a constant part of his extended family. This clothesline crossed from one side of a small mountain valley to the other. The far end of the line was strung from a giant Douglas fir, about 40 metres off the ground.

I looked at Ox's malfunctioning high-line and then at Ox. "Are you planning to log the place?" I asked.

Dead serious, Ox looked up and stared up to where the spar reached into the clouds. "This clothesline is for Marge."

Well, what could I do but volunteer to climb the spar tree and see if I could set the line back on the pulley? I wandered over to the far side of the little valley and began to climb. I climbed and climbed till I was high over the creek far below. When I looked down, Ox was a smiling ant.

From this grand vista I began to understand the expanse of his thinking. This was the art of utility at its best. A clothesline high enough to avoid the neighbour's irrigation system, high enough to catch the breeze that flows down a valley with a small, cool creek in its bottom. High enough to get the laundry up into the weather systems. And long enough to do all the laundry at once.

Even Christo, the installation artist, with his pink, plastic-wrapped islands and draped canyons could not hold a torch to this. It was a tribute to the greatest clothes dryer of all. A masterpiece!

I understood as Ox had stared down from this lofty platform the whole universe had shifted into place. He must have felt oneness with line, weather and utility. At some unnoticed moment a choice was made. Art over purpose. Invention over process. A fusion driven by experience that teaches us to fall in love with all that is wild and human.

High over the little valley, I settled myself onto a strong branch and with one arm desperately hugging the trunk of the spar, I reached out and slipped the wire onto the pulley.

Ox, who had returned to the carport platform, shot the clothesline around the pulley, pulling one lonely sock across the pasture to within a few metres of my high perch. I took this podiatrist's flag to mean a kind of truce had been reached with the problem. Then, cautious as a bear, I slowly backed down the full 40-metre length of the tree.

This gave Ox time to run across the little valley. He was waiting at the base of the tree when I descended. With a rather intense smile on his face, he reached out and shook my hand.

CHAPTER

8

Freddy's Saddle

FREDDY AND I WERE WALKING the back forty of his bench-land property at the base of Bear Mountain when I noticed he had an old saddle hanging on the back of one of his sheds.

On closer inspection, I recognized that this was a unique style of saddle, with steep forks and a high cantle. The forks of a saddle describe the shape of the tree, the part that meets the horse's back. In the past, a typical saddle horse had pronounced withers so the saddletree was shaped steeply to match the horse's conformation. The modern western saddle horse has been bred for a wider, flatter back, and the popularity of roping as a timed sport has dictated that the cantle, the rear portion of the saddle seat, be lowered so that roping contestants can slip off their horses quickly.

Mice had eaten the sheepskin, and the saddle was dried out with the leather starting to curl, but otherwise it was in near-perfect condition.

When I inquired about the saddle, Freddy drew back and examined me, peering down his sharp hawk-like nose, and said, "That saddle belonged to one of the Bugaboo sisters from Spillimacheen and has a lot of history attached to it."

I remembered briefly meeting the Bugaboo sisters when I first moved to the valley in the 1970s. They were a couple of old English gals living in a cabin upcountry with two dozen mutts. They were remnants from an early tourist boom that brought many young English couples of breeding, but limited means, to the valley to try their hand at creating estates. Most of the men went back to mother England to fight the Huns during the First World War, and their dreams of establishing estates died with them on the battlefields of Europe. Some of the women stayed and took up trapping, outfitting and ranching.

After further examination and discussion about the saddle, I inwardly decided that pack rats and mice should not eat an important piece of history like this. I asked Freddy if he would mind if I took the saddle home and cleaned it up for him.

He eyed me as if I was a teenage vandal or an outright thief, but finally, at my urging, we made a deal that I could use the saddle for a while in return for fixing it.

Freddy's Saddle

I was partly motivated by a desire to preserve the saddle, but was also curious to try out the older design and compare it with modern saddles.

Over the next few weeks I carefully took the old saddle apart. Everything was indeed in mint condition; it just needed some tender loving care. I checked the rawhide-wrapped tree for cracks and breaks, but everything was solid. I scrubbed each piece in the tub with saddle soap. As it dried, I massaged neatsfoots oil into it, bringing life into the leather.

I scrubbed the dirt from the keeper, a small tag of leather attached to the cantle of some saddles, and made out the name of the maker. It said Hutchings and Riley, Calgary, N.W.T. This meant the saddle was made before 1905, as Alberta did not become a province till then. This was a genuine "oldtimey" saddle, a piece of history.

As I worked the old leather to life and reassembled the saddle, I thought about how pleased Freddy would be to have this valuable antique in working condition again.

About a month after refinishing the saddle, I was in Whitefish, Montana, at a saddle shop when I noticed a new saddle sitting on a display stand. It had the same unusual rigging as the Hutchings and Riley. I learned from the maker that it was a Vesalius design with a Frank Moan (pronounced Mean) rigging. This style of saddle had originated out of Vesalius, Missouri, nearly a century ago.

I made a few minor sewing repairs around the horn and then had old Roy Barret, a part-time shoe and saddle repair man from Wilmer, sew a new sheepskin onto the underside of the skirts. Finally, the old saddle looked good, its dark leather shone a deep bronze colour, and with the repairs finished, it was ready for use.

I was anxious to try riding this old-style rigging. Its narrow forks fit our older, high-withered saddle horse, and I was pleased with the natural position one assumed in the saddle. It put the rider more forward than the modern style of saddle, but it was nevertheless very comfortable. I liked the narrow swells and slick fork and the way it put me in close contact with the horse. I think people rode sitting more upright in the old days. Many modern saddles imitate an easy chair in their design and tend to let the rider sit back, which should be avoided as it puts weight on the horse's kidneys and sets the rider back of the horse's centre of gravity.

I used the old saddle once in a while and enjoyed the fact that I had rehabilitated it, but finally the day came when Freddy wanted his saddle again.

I reluctantly threw the saddle in the truck and drove to his place on the benches. I had carefully polished it the evening before to have it looking good for Freddy.

I pulled it out of the back of the old red suburban, handed it to Freddy with a big smile and began telling him how I had taken it apart and washed the dirt out of it and oiled it with care.

But as I explained the details of my work I couldn't help notice that Freddy's expression was getting darker and darker. His face was finally so contorted that I stopped my explanation and asked, " What's the trouble, Fred?"

He scowled and said in a bitter tone, "You washed that saddle?"

"Yeah. I scrubbed the dirt off it so I could apply oil."

"You washed all the history out of it."

"What?" I asked, not comprehending his meaning.

"All that dirt and grime was put there by people who used that saddle. You washed all the history out of it!" exclaimed Freddy again, as if I had abused a sacred rite.

I turned an embarrassed red. A long silence and then I spluttered, "If you want it back the way it was I'll drag it behind the truck for a few miles so it will look historical again!"

There was an uncomfortable silence as Freddy took the saddle and walked back to the shed and hung it by one stirrup on the nail where it had rested untended for many years.

It was one of those times when nothing could be said or done to make things right. I learned the hard lesson, though, that people value things differently. And that ultimately one has to respect those differences even if it means letting an antique saddle get eaten by pack rats.

In the long run, Freddy and I didn't let it get between us. A few years later I was over at Freddy's and noticed the old Hutchings and Riley saddle still hanging behind the shed, dried out with the leather curled and cracking. The mice and pack rats had eaten most of the new sheepskin.

I didn't say a word.

CHAPTER

9

Eric's Tune-Up

ERIC WAS A LOCAL OUTFITTER who worked the Findlay
drainage in the Purcell Mountains of British Columbia. As a
park ranger, I would encounter him on the trails or in camp
during our travels. One day Eric related this story.

Eric had decided he would ride one of his young horses
on a supply trip up the Findlay. He was packing supplies into
the various camps and cabins during the summer to prepare for the fall outfitting season. It would be a good time to
get some miles on a young horse. As the trip progressed, the
colt he was riding kept fussing and turning sideways, refusing to head directly up the trail. Eric fought him most of the
trip to Frying Pan Camp, directing him forward with the
reins and urging him to move on.

Young horses are often this way when first put in the front of the line. It's a pretty traumatic situation; instead of being safely pulled behind old Freda steadily plodding up the trail, all of a sudden there are dark spooky stumps, waving alder, rushing streams and the overpowering scent of wild animals.

Being at the front exposes the trainees to many potential encounters, from bees to grizzlies. It is a challenging experience for them, and the rider must patiently control and direct the student horse so it can gain confidence and eventually become an intuitive leader. Some horses never do settle down and become good lead horses. The ones that do are highly prized among trail guides and nightriders.

After three hours of patient work, Eric had had enough! The colt was getting balkier as time went on, turning sideways, refusing to cross small obstacles and move up the trail. Eric stopped the pack string and tied up the balking horse. He announced to the entourage of pack horses and wranglers that he was going to "Tune up that son of a gun!"

Eric rummaged around in his saddlebags and got out a set of effective-looking spurs. He sat down next to a big spruce and carefully buckled them onto his boots. He strode with renewed confidence toward the colt. His spurs jangled on the rocky path. The colt's ears pricked back at the new sound. Eric untied the young horse and gave the lead shank to the pack string to a wrangler. He stuck one foot in the stirrup and swung assuredly into the saddle, picked up the reins and gave the horse a squeeze pointing him up the trail.

Again the colt began fussing, turning from side to side and refusing to make headway up the trail. Eric gave the horse a bump with the spurs. The colt felt the prick of the iron on his flanks and immediately tensed. Eric squeezed harder, giving the colt another touch with the spurs.

I don't know exactly what goes through a horse's mind the first time they feel the touch of a spur. I do know some horses lift up and focus, as if they understand that the rider is saying, "Pay attention!"

But I caution inexperienced riders that the spur is to be used lightly to get a horse's attention. Only rough-stock rodeo riders and bull riders actually use spurs to engage extreme responses in the beast they're sitting on. Spurs are best used as a gentle extension of the heel to give and clarify direction.

The colt Eric was riding, however, did not have such refined horse-whisperer notions about directions of travel, contact, communications and energy, and the instant the colt felt the touch of steel to his flank, he came undone.

He jumped straight up, bucking and tossing his rider backward, then jumped sideways with the dexterity of a prizewinning cutting horse. Eric hung on and was jolted forward with the thrust of the back end of the colt, just as the little horse threw its head back, smacking Eric smartly between the eyes.

If you've tried this connection, even at slow speed, you'll know that a horse's head is heavy and very bony. Eric rolled off the colt into the bush and lay still. The colt continued thrashing down the trail for a ways till it realized the danger had passed. The next pack horse in the line stood over Eric, perplexed by the stillness of the fallen contestant.

During these moments of silence many thoughts course through the witnesses' heads: "Did you see that horse twist?" "Did you see how that head came back?" "Glad that wasn't me!" "Sure hope he's not hurt too bad!" "Are you okay?"

Eric came to his senses and slowly sat up and shook the stardust from his head. He carefully reached down and felt his limbs. He unbuckled his spurs and struggled to his feet, brushing himself off, picking up his hat and testing various mechanical functions. He slowly straightened his glasses as the world came into focus.

Holding the spurs in his hand, he looked at the equine and human audience that had gathered around him and said laconically, "Well, I sure tuned him up."

Eric walked meekly down the trail and caught the colt. He put the spurs back in his saddlebag and then got on. As he rode up the trail in a fuzzy and less-ordered world, Eric was more or less content to let the colt fuss and find his own pace.

10

Gopher Paradise

JIM SMITH LAKE PARK IS a small but popular park encompassing a small benchland lake and pine forest. Typically, these lakes are surrounded by cattail bulrushes and willowed riparian areas. Because of its close proximity to Cranbrook, truckloads of sand and topsoil were hauled in and quick-growing and resilient Kentucky bluegrass planted to create a beach, play area and campground among the pines.

There was a growing wildlife problem at Jim Smith Lake, and the public was complaining. The intrepid gophers of the area were taking over the limited beach area by excavating burrows and building mounds. The sand made for easy digging, and the irrigated grass provided succulent forage for these homesteading rodents.

Gopher Paradise

What more could the highly sociable Columbia ground squirrel want? A shallow mountain lake with a view, good materials for making burrows and an abundance of cultured feed had created ideal habitat. Most of its natural predators such as coyote, fox, hawks, badgers and bears were shy of the area because of its proximity to the city. It was gopher paradise!

Parks must react to public complaints, and it was finally determined, given strong public opinion, that the gophers living there were not a cherished feature of biological diversity, but a pest.

Something had to be done! What if someone tripped in a gopher hole playing beach ball? They would sue. And all those mounds—soon there would be nothing but mounds. The complaints were heard. Though the public is often cynical about reaction by government agencies, the fact is complaints are taken very seriously, and there is even a tendency to overreact. And such was the case concerning said rodents. The problem of the pesky rodents was turned over to the area supervisor.

The area supervisor, in turn, called Rob, the area ranger. Area rangers have the interesting task of enacting whatever directive the regional office decides to implement. And Rob was the type of ranger who was eager to please and who would never admit that he did not have the answer to a problem, especially something as simple as getting rid of a few pesky gophers. Rob assured his supervisor that the

thing to do was to poison the little critters with rat poison—
strychnine.

"They do it all over. It will take of them," said Rob.

"Okay, Rob, take care of it."

It was an intensely hot June weekend at Jim Smith Lake
Park, the first really hot weather after a long, cold spring,
and the beach was crowded. Summer weather can be short
and fickle in the Kootenays, so on good days the local pop-
ulation heads to Jim Smith Lake in droves. People were
swimming, having picnics, sunbathing and fussing with
their dogs. Families with small children played leisurely on
the grass. Citizens seeking respite from Cranbrook strip
malls sat under their sun hats and stared blankly across
the small lake, letting this precious, lazy Saturday drift by
as slowly as possible.

It was late morning when someone noticed the first
dead gopher. It dragged itself out of its burrow, desperate for water, and began convulsions that culminated in a
heaving death.

Strychnine, derived from the seeds of a tree, *Strychnos
nux-vomica*, has been used as rat poison for five centuries.
It stimulates the spinal cord and increases secretion of gas-
tric juices, causing thirst, and is characterized by violent
convulsions.

One after another, gophers dragged themselves out of
their cool cellars to die, gasping beside their dirt mounds.
By noon, a host of dying gophers struggled out of burrows

in a desperate attempt to escape their fate, convulsing terribly and dying before the unbelieving public.

Someone called the Ministry of Environment, which responded quickly to the emergency by sending out a conservation officer, who immediately closed and evacuated the beach, then proceeded to assess the situation.

Why, all of a sudden, had the gophers of Jim Smith Lake hauled themselves out of their dens and died, in a park, no less? The conservation officer called the B.C. Parks office at Wasa. He was informed that a ranger was taking care of the gopher situation at the lake, and eventually it was revealed that rat poison spilled into their holes on Friday night had killed the gophers.

Rob seemed unperturbed by the situation; after all, he had taken care of the gopher problem. The area supervisor was nervously waiting for a call from the press, who had been alerted to the situation, probably through their constant scan of police radio channels.

Conservationists and beach-goers were outraged and demanded an explanation from the district manager. He was quoted in the *Cranbrook Daily News* the next day as saying, "It is a challenge to find the right balance between conservation and recreation."

Amen.

CHAPTER

11

Hungry Hank

HUNGRY HANK IS WHAT we called him. The name came from young Mahoney, who worked faithfully for Hank for a few years on the Findlay Creek hunting territory. The story goes that Hank rode into base camp with a hunter and says to Mahoney, "What's for supper?"

Mahoney goes into the cook-tent and comes out with a box of Red River cereal, a staple in all of Hank's camps, pours some into a bowl, hands it to Hank and says, "*You* cook it!" Mahoney steps into the stirrup, swings his leg over his saddle horse and pulls out, never to be seen on the Findlay again.

Hank would have had that deeply furrowed frown on his sharp, weathered face. His massive curved eyebrows would have narrowed for a few moments and then in an unperturbed way, he would have cracked another twenty-six of Windsor Deluxe rye whisky and made the best of the situation by delegating some other hapless wrangler to cook up some grub.

Any trip with Hank guaranteed adventure. There was always a shortage of something and always a surplus of whisky. If the weather was dirty and miserable, heroic effort kept us dry under ragged old tents covered with layers of 2 mil poly, or late starts made for long night rides. I recall an incident where a wrangler turned the horses onto the slide above camp, as he thought no one would possibly be arriving five hours after dark. About midnight Hank rode in with an outfit. His loaded pack horses heard the horse bells up on the slide and immediately broke off from the string and tore up the slide, dumping gear and groceries far and wide.

The stories of wilderness adventure would expand to daring and grand proportions. Sagas of survival would drift down the creek and back into the States with the American clients who would retell the misadventures and adventures at hunting clubs over bourbon and cigars. Hank's well-deserved reputation as a raconteur and guide would bring even more work-weary pilgrims intent on the great North American elk safari.

During one particularly rugged bit of weather, I pitched a lean-to made of an orange plastic tarp above my sleeping bag, underneath one of Hank's leaky, aged canvas edifices.

The tent flaps had torn away, and the camp inside the tent was easily seen from the main corral. Hank observed the set-up and asked, "What is that about?"

When I explained that I intended to stay dry, Hank, to my surprise, did not see the humour or the practicality in this and appeared insulted by this obvious lack of show on my part. He remarked that such faithless preventative measures would only invite more bad weather!

As insurance against inviting a weather calamity, Hank sent me to the Middle Fork with a new guide, Jerome, and a couple of hunters to remove the hunting camp that had been set up for the season. The idea was to hunt our way down the main valley, stay for a day or two on the Middle Fork and then make our way to Pack Out, where the trucks were parked at the end of the road. Jerome was a precocious 17-year-old from Canal Flat on his first wrangling job. He had been tutored by his father in the ways of the bush from an early age. We started the ride late in the afternoon, having been assured that camp was set up and that provisions were cached at the Middle Fork Camp.

"Everything you need is up there!" said Hank, as we swung our legs over the saddles and pointed down the valley with pack horses and clients in tow. Evening was the best time for hunting. If we were lucky we would take an elk on the way to the Middle Fork, so named because the trail up the headwall started midway between the first camp at Frying Pan and the base camp at Caribou. By the time we reached the Middle Fork junction from the main trail, we were about halfway there and it was dark.

We did lots of night riding on the Findlay. The usual practice while hunting was to hide at the bottom of a slide path until darkness had descended into the valley and watch for the elusive elk to appear, which they often did late in the evening after the cool downwinds put them on the move. Sometimes the return ride to base camp was so charcoal black you couldn't see your hand in front of your face. You put your trust in the horses, gave them their heads and ambled back to camp on a long rein, the horses shuffling along with their noses about an inch from the ground, snorting and snuffling and seemingly able to navigate by smell as easily as if it were light.

This is where a good broad-brimmed cowboy hat proved its worth. I could duck my head and shield my face to keep branches and sticks out of my eyes and prevent bushels of evergreen needles from finding their way down my shirt collar and into my long underwear.

One black night I trailed a hunter from the upper meadows on the Middle Fork to camp. Although a preacher by profession and presumably with the creator on his side to protect him, he began to cry, terrified that we would be lost forever in the wilderness and then eaten. As I often did while riding in the dark, I sang the song "The Night Rider's Lament," to keep me and the horses company, safe from bears and to calm the preacher:

Why do you ride for your money
Why do you rope for short pay
You ain't gettin' nowhere
And you're losin' your share
Boy, you must have gone crazy out there
But he's never seen the Northern Lights
Never seen a hawk on the wing
He's never seen Spring hit the Great Divide
And never heard Ol' Camp Cookie sing

It had been over a year since I had ridden the trail to the Middle Fork Camp; however, once the usual anxiety of the coming darkness passed, we settled in and let the horses find the trail up the headwall with its thirteen creek crossings. The moon rose briefly, casting a useable light for a time, and then it disappeared behind a thick layer of cloud, returning us to the blackness of a trail meandering deep in the forest at night. A cold rain pelted down, making the trail slick and treacherous. Each unseen branch unloaded a bucket of water on me; I began to fantasize about dry tents and the fast warmth of glowing tin heaters.

The previous year I had guided two hunts from this camp. Hank, Freddy, Yvonne and I had ridden in ahead of the guiding season during the late summer to set things up. We put up a couple of wall tents, cached some canned goods in a bag hanging high up in a tree and then cut and split a starter pile of dry firewood. However, Freddy, Hank's lead guide, was no longer working the Findlay, and I would come to realize just how much Hank had depended on Freddy to organize and outfit the remote camps.

We finally broke out of the heavy timber into an opening along the fast-tumbling little creek. In the darkness, I had nearly missed the camp. There were no tents! I reached into my saddlebag for a flashlight and shone the beam around the clearing. A couple of sets of pack boxes lay open on their sides and bits of food wrapping and plastic floated around the site. It looked as though a hungry bear had scavenged the camp. A couple of ragged canvas tarps lay in a rumpled heap near the campfire ring.

We dismounted and tied the horses to nearby trees, then scrounged dejectedly through the cache. A squirrel ran out of one of the boxes with a bit of tinfoil in its mouth, then clambered up into a nearby tree and set up a mocking chatter. Enthusiastically I announced that I had found a Coleman lantern that could shed some light on matters, and then we'd get the camp sorted out. What a godsend for working in this blackness! At least we'd see to unsaddle and unpack the horses, get them hobbled and across the creek out of the way, and then we'd manufacture a dry place to sleep and hopefully something to eat.

The flashlight gave out. Jerome kept lighting matches to provide enough light so I could see to fuel and pump the lantern. We huddled under a tarp out of the wind and rain as I mounted a new mantle to the stem and carefully burned it off. When all was ready I moved into the open and turned the control valve, struck a fresh match and with cold, stiffened fingers stuck it through the hole into the combustion chamber.

The lantern burst into fiery mass! The raging ball of expanding, hot yellow flame fed on pressurized naphtha. I hurled the cantankerous fiery monster into the creek, and it was followed by a spontaneous stream of curses. The lantern clattered across the stones into the water making a kind of "phitt" sound. A glare of flame drifted down the creek then disappeared, plunging us once again into the stormy, wet darkness.

With the lantern safely stowed at the bottom of the creek, we fumbled about in the darkness unpacking and unsaddling the horses. As I undid the saddles, I carefully folded the latigo straps and tied them in place with a saddle knot. Hank had taught me to do this so the latigos would be easy to find in case I was ever saddling horses in the dark! I belled a couple of horses, hobbled the bunch and sent them across the creek in a cavalcade of clanging bells and jingling hobbles onto an avalanche slide path to feed.

The first and most holy rule of working with animals is that they are looked after first. Then clients, then yourself. I had learned that animals came first early in life, when growing up on a bush farm.

Jerome proved himself able and soon scrounged enough wood and built a fire. The rain let up and a half moon

appeared between clumps of racing clouds. We found a tin
pot and boiled water to which we added a partially eaten
package of chicken noodle soup that had survived the
maelstrom. This went down with the sandwiches I had
packed before we left Caribou Camp. Pulling the pack boxes
into a half circle in front of the fire, we rigged last year's tent
poles into a lean-to. Jerome and I tied the patchy old tarps
over the crude frame with binder twine. That was another
thing Hank had suggested, "Always stuff extra binder twine
in your saddlebags."

After weighting the edges of the tarps with rocks, we
set the saddles at the back of the lean-to as pillows, then
laid saddle pads and horse blankets on the ground to make
sleeping pads. We laid out our sleeping bags, put our rain
gear over the end of the bags, and the four of us shimmied
into the confined space.

As we settled into our makeshift shelter, we watched
the orange flames of the campfire lick the coming rain. The
soup and sandwiches had taken the edge off our hunger.
Further up the valley, a wolf howled. An elk bugled far in
the distance. Horse bells were ringing steadily as the hungry
beasts tore off rich mouthfuls of succulent grasses and forbs.
Frost nipped our noses. Lord only knows what the hunters
thought. We were too exhausted to care much, but we were
dry and fed, high in the hills.

I guess I had expected that a cozy camp would be set
up as it had been the previous year. I watched the flames. A

vision of Hank pointing to boxes of turnips, carrots, cab-bages, potatoes and canned goods in the basement of his Fort Steele home drifted by as I fell asleep. At the time, I had smiled in the unfounded assumption that Hank, the head guide, the cook, or someone would have transported these supplies to the various camps.

We were tired but had made it through another day in the hills, and although there had been a few shortfalls in the camp department, tomorrow we would sort things out, maybe find something in the old food cache, maybe kill an elk. Life was good!

Even though it rankled me at the time that the camps were in such rough condition, I did learn to look after others with a package of chicken noodle soup, a half-eaten piece of cheese, an old sandwich, binder twine and a few ragged tarps. I learned that you look after your camp and grub and that attitude is everything; mind you, it is nice to have some stuff to work with.

* * *

One fine June afternoon, Yvonne and I drove into Hank's place just off Highway 95 near Fort Steele. "Campsall Arabians Outfitting" read the sign on the ranch's gate. After enquiring as to Hank's whereabouts at the house, we were directed to three people working on a fenceline near the barns. I stepped out of the truck and walked down to the fence, stuck out my hand and shook hands with Hank.

Pointing to the truck, I said Yvonne and I were looking for a guiding job. Hank turned to the young couple he had been instructing on the repair of the fence and handed over a hammer, saying, "You change the oil in this thing; I'm going up to the house for a minute."

The bewildered young fellow took the hammer, looking at it as if there might indeed be a place to change the oil on a hammer. He stood staring at the hammer as we made our way along the fence leading to the road, barn and house.

At the house we met Artha Rose, Hank's wife (known affectionately as the Queen Bee), and Freddy, the lead hand. We also met Artha's pet skunk as it bolted through the back door into the kitchen, scaring the daylights out of us before it took up its usual residence behind the fridge. We passed an enjoyable afternoon over a bottle of Windsor Deluxe and made a pact to join Hank and Freddy, Hank's head guide, on a trip into the Middle Fork during late August to cut trail and set up camps for the coming fall hunts.

On the appointed day, Yvonne and I left home early in the morning and made the journey up the truck-killing Findlay Creek logging road, turned off at the bridge and bounced and heaved our way up an old spur road another 11 kilometres to Valentine Camp, or Pack Out, as it was known. Valentine Camp had been a horse loggers' camp in the olden days. A large wild meadow and a good clear-running creek, a tributary to the Findlay, as well as its location near the trailhead, made this an ideal place for starting out.

Yvonne and I rolled into Pack Out about 10 a.m. We parked the truck and walked over to the bunkhouse where Hank was bent over, shoeing the hind foot of a horse. A wire and pole corral reached back into the larch forest toward the creek, where a small band of about eight horses stood dozing in the shade, back legs cocked and tails swishing at flies. An old bunkhouse framed of rough-cut two-by-sixes and sided and roofed with wane-edge fir stood in an opening in the forest, just off the bush road. The planks on the cabin had blackened and cupped from years of weather; occasionally the dark wood was livened by a swirl of red or gold where the sun had mellowed the sapwood. A few cribbed feed boxes nailed to skinny pine trees hung askew, and a hitching rail ran lengthwise nailed between two trees near the front of the cabin.

Hank looked up briefly from his work. "There's two things you should never learn to do, Christensen: one is shoe horses and the other is run a chainsaw." Words to live by; however, I had to become intimate with both in order to live and work in the mountain backcountry.

Saddle horses, pack animals, outfitting, guiding. Finally, the real thing! We turned up the valley at the end of the old logging trail, away from the cutbanks and stumps. A sweet, wild, pungent pine and balsam scent carried by cold glacial air rushed down Findlay Creek and poured over us like salvation.

My thoughts drifted back to the previous summer when I was working in "The Valley" on construction projects, building basements in the intense, dirty heat of the valley summer. A fine powder drifted in the air from the drying concrete forms and filled the lime-impregnated air as I marched around a newly poured basement in the 40°C heat, snapping form ties with a sledge hammer and then lifting wet four-by-eight-foot plywood forms into a stack to ready them for the next job.

The fact was I hated construction work, and though I tried hard to make the best of it because it would teach me the skills necessary to build a house, I took little pleasure in it and did not find particular joy in doing it just right. One stifling day I crawled out of the pit and collapsed in the shade against the cool side of a sweating concrete wall to drink some water and eat a dry sandwich. I looked across the dusty construction site at the snow-capped mountains and wild green valleys leading out of the Rocky Mountain Trench. I told myself, "Either I find a job in the hills or I leave!"

The next day I was framing an expansive floor on a new commercial building in downtown Invermere. The basement walls were built five inches out of square, and the job was going badly. When the boss, who had built the basement, came on site and tried to help, I lost it. He was working below me, and slowly an argument heated up. Before long I was hopping back and forth on the open floor joists yelling about the stupid walls being out of square. He was yelling at me to work with it, all of which was amusing to the rest of the crew and possibly a few bystanders.

By the time I reached the end of the 100-foot building and stepped onto the sidewalk, I had quit. I unbuckled the heavy belt full of hammers, utility knife, tape measures, nail puller, nails, chalk line and assorted squares, threw it into the back of my bright orange 1962 Fargo van and drove down to the beach. I waded into the water, swam out to the floating dock, hauled myself up on it and looked up toward the peaks—I had been baptized in the sacred headwaters. I did not pick up a hammer for hire for many years.

The decision to find work in the backcountry as a guide changed my life and set it on a profound and changing course. For the next 15 years I guided for various outfits as far north as the Wernecke Mountains and Bonnet Plume in the northeast Yukon to the Rocky Mountains in northern Montana.

So here I was a year later, riding into the wild Purcell Mountains, the "hills," as Hank called them. By nightfall, we reached Frying Pan Camp. Freddy hobbled and turned out the horses. Yvonne stared into a pack box, not sure how to prepare dinner for four hungry riders with these limited ingredients. She looked at Freddy and back into the box. Freddy graciously suggested combining Kraft dinner with a can of corn and a can of tomatoes. Canned tuna on the side. "Tastes great!"

Hank and I put up a lean-to, and before long we had settled in front of a blazing fire wolfing down the "special" and talking about the fall guiding season. A heavy dew settled over the camp. We were at peace with the white noise of Findlay Creek rushing down the boulder-strewn channel beside us. A moose clattered out of the creek and trotted down the horse trail.

Starting early in the morning, we rode to the Middle Fork Camp and set up a couple of wall tents, each with a tin wood heater. The days were long, so we cut and stacked a starter supply of firewood, then rode up the narrow hanging valley, cutting out the trail above the camp as we made our way to the big wet meadows marking the divide between the Skookumchuck and the Findlay drainage. Hank talked about how to hunt this valley, cautioning me to be patient in accessing the narrow valley leading to the upper end of the Middle Fork. "Don't head up to the slides until evening when the wind starts to blow down or you may as well ride up the valley blowing a trumpet."

The first two hunters I guided into the Middle Fork owned Datsun car dealerships. They had met at a sales conference in Minnesota, become friends and decided to go hunting together. Roly was from Minnesota and Charles from Georgia. They were "good hunters." After some years of guiding, I would savvy the term "good hunters." "Good hunters" understood that this was fair-chase hunting and not shooting fish in barrel. Bad hunters were people who could not really afford to do what they were doing, and for them to come home empty-handed was a great loss of face and reputation. They inevitably turned sour. Roly and

Charles enjoyed each other's company and appreciated the effort that Yvonne and I made for them. Roly shot an elk mid-hunt, a good 300-yard shot, well placed, and the animal went down where he stood.

I packed up Roly's elk meat the next day and made the 18-hour return trip to Pack Out, where someone would take the meat to Canal Flat to hang it in a freezer. Upon my return, I ventured that we should climb the avalanche path across from camp and walk into the basin to the east. It would mean a night out, so I organized some rough backpacking outfits out of feedbags and rope. We took just enough food for a couple of days, a tarp, sleeping pads, extra jackets and rain gear.

Charles was from a humble background; his father was a bathtub enameller. A heavy man with a southern aristocratic air, he spoke of hunting quail on grand plantations, so I called him Mr. Charles, which I believe he liked. It took most of the afternoon and evening to gain 600 metres of elevation. We moved very slowly and rested often. Eventually we were able to look down on our camp far below and see the expanse of the country.

We scouted the basin to the east without success, but toward evening found a small, mossy, level area where we could spread out our tarps and rest. We ate canned sardines and bread and drank water from a small, cool spring nearby. Darkness descended and we crawled under the tarp on top of a nest of thick moss.

One of the intrigues of guiding was that the "good hunters" became your best friends for 10 days. They were mostly from places I knew nothing about, and sometimes they shared stories from home. I was interested in how other people live, and Mr. Charles had a philosophic nature and loved to tell a story: "I had a good ole boy, a black man, who worked for me as a gardener for many years. He was old style; he would never come and sit with white folks. If we invited him, which we often did, to take a break from his hot work and join us for an iced tea, he would always decline sitting at the table, saying, 'No thanks, Mr. Charles, I'll just have a drink. I'm just fine.' He would come to the table, take his iced tea and then sit on a step not far away.

"He was the 'help,' and we were the 'owners,' and he never would cross that line. But one day he came to me and he said, 'Mr. Charles, I have been working for you a long time and I believe I have done a good job. Now my boy, he is in jail over in the next county, and he's been shot and no one there will help him. I know he was wrong. He was beating his woman and she shot him all right. Now he's bleeding to death in that jail and there is nobody that can help him. The sheriff over there, he won't bring in the doctor.'

"I said I would do what I could but didn't know how much success I would have because in our counties the sheriff is elected. Influence and political sway doesn't migrate from one county to another. So I phoned up the sheriff and I said to him, 'Now I don't want you to start believing that

I am overstepping my ground and am a lover of the black man, but that boy you've got in your jail cell that's bleedin' to death, he's the son of my man that works in my garden, and he has been a good ole boy. So if you would, I would appreciate it if you could bring him in a doctor. I'll pay for it.' And so the sheriff did do that and the boy lived. But you see how I had to approach this thing? That's what it's like in Georgia, if you want to do a good thing for a black man. If I lectured that sheriff about civil rights, the boy would have bled to death for sure. The laws have changed in Georgia but you are still dealing with people."

There was a long silence as we lay on the side of the mountain looking at the heavens. The Milky Way swept across the heavens like gravel fanned out on the curve of a broad mountain stream. I pointed out the Great Bear and the North Star. Suddenly a small star moved quickly and deliberately across the night sky.

"What was that?" Charles exclaimed in an alarmed voice.

"Just a satellite. The sun is reflecting off it."

"You mean we can *see* satellites?"

It was a revelation to him! He was an urban dweller who had rarely seen the night sky and was truly astounded. I understood a lesson about guiding that night—that the real challenge and satisfaction in guiding is to bring someone safely to a place they thought they could never go, and then to relive with them the wonder of seeing something for the first time.

* * *

There is a fair bit of bullshit that goes along with running and marketing an outfit. It's part of the business. At Pack Out after a trip, I've listened to hunters knowingly compare stories or "lies" they had been told. In fact, there seemed to be prestige attached to who could come up with the biggest piece of bona fide bullshit. And Hank was a master.

Hank told me he always liked to keep a paint horse around. Paints have a negative/positive colour scheme, and it can be difficult to tell one from another. He said they were the best horses for resale.

"Why is that?" I asked.

"Well you see, last year I sold a paint horse to a fella over in Kimberley for his daughter. He had the horse for about a week but it ran away. In fact, it swam across the Kootenay River which was in full flood and came right back here. So I put it in the corral.

"The fellow who had bought the horse called me after awhile and asked me if I didn't have another paint horse for sale. The last one had run off and his daughter was heart-broken about the missing horse. I told him I was sorry about the lost horse and hoped it had not drowned in the river. But I did have a similar animal, a brother to the first in fact, and I would make him a special deal on it because of his previous purchase and his daughter's sadness.

"About a week later, this fella came by and looked at the horse. He was easily convinced that this was the brother to the horse I sold him a couple of weeks ago. In fact, he looked so much like the first horse he was sure his daughter would not be able to tell the difference. So he bought him, at a good price, of course. About a week later, that same horse was back in my yard. But you know, I felt sorry for the guy and phoned him and told him he should come and get his horse."

I had grown used to Hank's bullshitting; it was just part of the business, and the way I looked at it was as long as he didn't involve me, what did I care? After a time though, one grows weary of it, especially if you are the object.

I had taken a hunter up the south slope of Barn Mountain to hunt goats. As we climbed the broad shoulder of the mountain, we crossed an old pack trail that led up at a steady pace. It soon became apparent that it was no ordinary trail. Extensive rockwork filled the gullies, and by the steady grade it was obvious the trail made possible the carrying of heavy loads by pack animals in very steep terrain.

There were many rumours the Blake brothers, long ago deceased, found a deposit of high-grade ore somewhere on the Findlay and had packed loads of rich galena ore to the new railway completed along the Upper Columbia Valley in 1915. According to legend, the Blake brothers were conscientious objectors from the First World War who had hidden on the lower benches of Findlay Creek and lived out their lives in this remote part of the Rockies, prospecting and ranching a few cattle.

Hungry Hank

During the 1860s, significant deposits of gold were sluiced from Wild Horse Creek, near Fort Steele, about 95 kilometres south of the Findlay. The famous Sullivan Mine at nearby Kimberley operated for nearly 100 years, primarily producing lead, zinc and silver. At one time it was the largest producer of galena in the British Empire. After the railroad was laid through the Rockies by Chinese labourers, legend had it that a small village of Chinese had prospered on the lower Findlay canyons, digging gold nuggets and fines (powdery gold flecks) lodged in the cracks of the river bed.

The Purcell Mountain Range, of which the Findlay is a major drainage, is millions of years older than the Rocky Mountains that run northwest/southeast on the east side of the Rocky Mountain Trench. The Purcells' steep, v-shaped valleys and rounded ridges are worn down by time and weather and reveal many small deposits of high-grade ore. In modern times, the Purcells are of major interest to prospectors looking for the other half of the Sullivan Mine. Hank was well aware of the Blake legacy.

As my hunter and I broke out of the trees into the alpine, the sculpted trail continued its upward climb into a small, high basin. There we found lengths of old rusting cable, iron wheels and scoops: parts of a cable-car system typically used to bring ore from a high point on a steep ridge or cliff face to a landing in the basin.

My plan was to climb into the next basin to the west, from where we would drop back down to the Findlay. Upon reaching the ridge dividing the basins, I found old claim markers. I picked up a hand-sized chunk of dark rock flecked with dark, silvery angular particles. It was heavy. This was the old Blake mine!

I shoved the ore in my pack, made a mental note of the location and continued the descent into the western basin, where we spent the night in the open under a tarp. We awoke under a skiff of snow the next day, descended to the valley floor, then followed the Findlay down to Pack Out.

Yvonne, my partner, had been holding down the fort at Pack Out. Paul (the hunter) and I arrived at midday. I told Yvonne I had found the old Blake Mine, but we should keep it quiet. However, being young and stupid, and feeling I needed to prove myself to Hank, I hauled out the piece of ore and dumped it on the table. I described how and where I had found the old mining gear and claim markers and then speculated that perhaps I should restake the claim. Pete, an old friend of Hank's, was also there.

The rules of the prospecting game are such that if a claim has not been worked for three years, then someone else can restake the claim. The Blake claim had been deserted for nearly half a century.

Hank took the piece of ore, examined it carefully, then placed it on the windowsill. He said it was low-grade stuff and that restaking old claims was just a lot of expense and work for nothing. These mines were everywhere, and the reason they were deserted was that they were worthless.

He then sent Paul and me to hunt from Caribou Camp, nine hours' ride upriver on the Findlay. Yvonne told me that later the next day, Pete came back and stopped in for coffee, saying he was waiting for Hank to pick him up. Hank was on his way to the heliport in Fairmont and would pick him up at the big meadow. He and Hank were flying up to Barn Mountain to stake the claim. Pete waited about three hours. Hank never did show, but Yvonne heard the helicopter fly over and go into the basin on the side of the mountain. The lure of the metal got the best of him, and Hank flew in and staked the claim himself.

Some years later, I worked on a land-use planning initiative and saw that Cominco, one of the largest mining companies in the country, now owned the Blake deposit.

Next hunt, I was in a bad mood. I knew I'd been taken advantage of, but had no one to blame but myself. We were taking three hunters and supplies into Caribou Camp. Hank and I had readied the pack string and some riding horses for the ride in. I had overheard Hank telling the hunters some bullshit hunting story, and he brought me into the conversation to verify the "facts," which I reluctantly did.

As was Hank's custom, he asked me to ride in front and lead the pack animals. He would bring up the rear and make sure the hunters were looked after. I swung onto the roan mare and picked up the lead shank of the first pack horse. I gave the mare a kick and headed up the trail. As we moved along, I urged the little horse forward and tugged on the pack horse's lead shank. I continued to press the gang forward at a fast walk. I chewed on what Hank had said and done and continued to push the rate of travel.

When we reached Frying Pan Camp we stopped to stretch and check the packs. The horses were hot and impatient. Hank made his way up to the front of the line. By this time, I was determined to say something about him not involving me in his bullshit.

"Hank. You can bullshit the troops all you want. But don't ask me verify it! I don't like it!"

Hank looked at me with a surprised but angry scowl and said, "You can be pissed off at me if you want, but don't take out your anger on the horses. Those horses work hard and have to last the whole season. You slow down and let them find the pace."

* * *

Freddy rounded up the last bunch of horses and equipment, mounted up the hunters and placed them into a lineup for the trip to Frying Pan Camp, about four hours up the trail. There had been many long days of preparation prior to the trip. Hank had spent a good part of this day entertaining the various client groups by helping them celebrate their departure up the trail. The last person to get in the saddle was Hank. He led Buck, a handsome, roman-nosed, palomino gelding, and placed him in the middle of the string. He tied Buck's reins so they would hang over the saddle horn and then swung backwards into the saddle. Hank folded his arms across his chest and let his head sag. As the outfit moved out onto the trail, he fell into a slumber that would last most of the next four hours.

Hank claimed Buck was such an intelligent trail horse that at the passing of any junction of the trail where they had taken another direction in the past, Buck would pause briefly to ask whether or not he wished to go up that trail again. Hank slumbered up and down through the steep sides of the Findlay Canyon, past Clear Creek and then through the lower end of the Jackpine Jungle till we hit the drift fence below Frying Pan. As we approached Frying Pan Camp and stopped to take down the drift fence, he changed his position and rode Buck into camp. He sprang down from his horse and did a little jig. "Well boys, we better get a camp made and some supper on."

As the evening skies darkened, we feasted on Kraft dinner mixed with fried hamburger and onions. We stretched a big tarp over a frame to form a lean-to in front of the fire. Freddy, Hank, the two hunters and I burrowed into our sleeping bags under the tarp.

As we began to doze, I heard one of the hunters ask Hank in as sincere a way as possible why he rode that horse sitting backwards. Hank guffawed and answered in a matter-of-fact tone, "Well, you wouldn't want to get a stick in your eye!"

12

Elk

ONE EARLY JULY DAY, JOE and I were riding toward Wigmore Lake, situated in a high pass about 60 kilometres north of Banff. We had finished some corral and fence work at Scotch Creek Warden Station on the Red Deer River during the last days of our shift. There is a large pasture at Scotch Camp, enclosed by a rail fence, and a set of corrals near the barn. The other Banff warden stations had similar set-ups with at least a set of corrals and a drift fence. Most of them were built many years ago, so Joe and I were slowly replacing them as we moved from station to station over the summers.

We had got up for an early start, as we had ahead of us at least a nine-hour ride down the abandoned Cascade Fire Road to Banff and the home corrals. The weather had changed yesterday, from a few hot days of sun and clear nights to a sultry atmosphere. During the night, heavy weather rolled in. We looked up at the low, dark clouds hanging in the pass as we prepared to leave. We checked our packs and tack and put an extra vest in our saddlebags in case it snowed, as it is prone to do every month of the year in the high mountains. Though summer storms are usually short in duration, they can bring fierce cold and wet conditions.

Wigmore Lake is in a high pass called Snow Creek. The old fire road traverses a wooded mountain above Scotch Camp on the Red Deer River and then climbs toward the pass. As we started to climb, the first heavy flakes drifted and swirled around us. The wind licked at the horses' manes and tails.

Setting a brisk pace, we tucked our slickers tightly around our legs and fanned them out over the back of the saddles to keep the snow off and to gather some heat from the horses. The sideways storm drifted snow into the cracks and gullies of our slickers and in around our necks. We tipped our hats toward the storm and hunkered down in the saddle.

With a few glances to the rear and a silent thank you to Wasp for not bucking me off on such a cold-backed morning, I could see we were packed right and could make good time. We were headed up over the aptly named Snow Creek Summit, after which we would drop down to Windy, Cuthead and Stoney warden stations, then on to Banff.

I pushed the horses a little. After a half hour of warm-up and urging, we were up to the steady, fast-paced walk we used to get quickly from one camp to another. It is a stretched-out rhythm the whole string can hold, and once you are in it you make good time.

We had just settled into this travelling rhythm when I noticed something big moving in the thick, tall alders along the creek below us. The first image that comes to my mind when seeing three-metre-high willows waving like grass in the wind is *Ursus arctos* crashing out of the brush to eat the pack string or possibly me. By the amount of commotion in those willows it had to be something big.

A couple of centimetres of snow had collected between the saddle horn and me, and I didn't really feel like changing my position in case that snowdrift ended up underneath my seat. Wasp was in a travelling frame of mind so we just kept going and watching. Whatever was in the gully began moving with us.

As we climbed along the old fire road, the thick willows and alder in the creek bed began to thin. A gust of wind swept across the trail and into the gully, clearing the drifting snow for a moment. We peered into the storm and saw a group of massive bull elk move out of the thick brush and up the slope in front of us. They got a good sniff of us, stopped, and stared.

The lead bulls threw back their dark heads, nostrils flared as they pulled lungfuls of thick, snow-filled mountain

128

air into their chests. Their bellies expanded and heaved and a hot steamy plume blew out of their nostrils into the cold air. The falling snow had formed a crust of ice along their dark manes and back.

They grunted and started to move across the fire road upslope toward the sparse timber above us. One, two, three and finally a dozen massive bulls, all six points or better, hustled out of the blinding storm, heads thrown back, glistening ivory-tipped antlers trailing along their backs.

We stopped and watched this regal parade as they trotted past, single file. Not moving their heads and massive antlers, they rolled their eyes toward us as they passed. The unmistakable elk-musk, urine-stink of them filled our senses. The horses sucked in the scent and stiffened as they nervously snorted and pawed the ground.

The bulls faded in and out of the blinding storm, sometimes visible, sometimes not. As they gained the sparse timber on higher ground, the last bull stopped momentarily to turn his head and see if they were being followed, then disappeared. The snow drifted down in great chunks as if the heavens had opened and covered their tracks as quickly as they had been made. There was no sign of them.

The restless pack string, Wasp, Quark, Tip, Zelda, Dale and my partner, Joe, had come to a standstill. We had all watched this rare display in mutual awe, witnesses to a rare sight. These majestic beasts were a great poem or a masterful piece of music, one you never forget, one you remember pieces of at unexpected times. The image was burned into our memories as fire burns a valley.

We moved on, taking a rare glimpse of paradise with us.

Index

Acknowledgements

I wish to acknowledge and thank the many people who work for the protection and preservation of our wilderness areas.

I also wish to acknowledge the support and love that my wife, Yvonne, has given me. She has travelled many days with me in the backcountry and is a true and fine wilderness companion.

About the Author

Peter Christensen grew up on a west-central Alberta bush farm before the oil rush. He graduated from university and then moved to the wilderness country, where he worked as a guide, a remote area lead hand for Banff National Park, and a backcountry and north coast provincial park ranger. He has published four books of poetry with Thistledown Press. His most recent poetry book is *Winter Range*, published in 2001.

More Great Books in the Amazing Stories Series

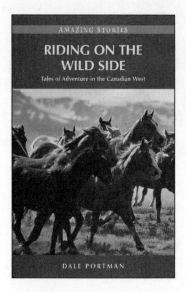

Riding on the Wild Side

Tales of Adventure in the Canadian West

Dale Portman

(ISBN 978-1-894974-80-6)

This collection of stories about working horses and the people who make a living riding them in Canada's mountain national parks suggests how eventful and adventurous life on horseback can be. Imagine chasing a herd of wild horses, galloping at full speed toward an impenetrable forest, and you get a sense of the excitement of the backcountry life. With nearly 30 years spent working in Jasper, Banff, Yoho and Glacier/Revelstoke national parks, retired warden Dale Portman has saddlebags stuffed with just such stories. *Riding on the Wild Side* shares some of his best.

Visit www.heritagehouse.ca to see the entire list of books in this series.